# Lecture Notes in Computer Science 16151

Founding Editors

Gerhard Goos
Juris Hartmanis

Editorial Board Members

Elisa Bertino, *Purdue University, West Lafayette, IN, USA*
Wen Gao, *Peking University, Beijing, China*
Bernhard Steffen, *TU Dortmund University, Dortmund, Germany*
Moti Yung, *Columbia University, New York, NY, USA*

The series Lecture Notes in Computer Science (LNCS), including its subseries Lecture Notes in Artificial Intelligence (LNAI) and Lecture Notes in Bioinformatics (LNBI), has established itself as a medium for the publication of new developments in computer science and information technology research, teaching, and education.

LNCS enjoys close cooperation with the computer science R & D community, the series counts many renowned academics among its volume editors and paper authors, and collaborates with prestigious societies. Its mission is to serve this international community by providing an invaluable service, mainly focused on the publication of conference and workshop proceedings and postproceedings. LNCS commenced publication in 1973.

Ruifeng Xu · Yirui Wu · Huan Chen · Ting Jin ·
Fahmy Ferdian Dalimarta · Liang-Jie Zhang
Editors

# AI and Multimodal Services – AIMS 2025

14th International Conference
Held as Part of the Services Conference Federation, SCF 2025
Hong Kong, China, September 27–30, 2025
Proceedings

*Editors*
Ruifeng Xu 
Harbin Institute of Technology
Shenzhen, Guangdong, China

Huan Chen
SF Technology Co., Ltd.
Shenzhen, China

Fahmy Ferdian Dalimarta
Universitas Muhammadiyah Tegal
Tegal, Indonesia

Yirui Wu
Hohai University
Nanjing, China

Ting Jin
Hainan University
Haikou, China

Liang-Jie Zhang 
Shenzhen University
Shenzhen, China

ISSN 0302-9743   ISSN 1611-3349 (electronic)
Lecture Notes in Computer Science
ISBN 978-3-032-08556-6   ISBN 978-3-032-08557-3 (eBook)
https://doi.org/10.1007/978-3-032-08557-3

© The Editor(s) (if applicable) and The Author(s), under exclusive license
to Springer Nature Switzerland AG 2026

This work is subject to copyright. All rights are solely and exclusively licensed by the Publisher, whether the whole or part of the material is concerned, specifically the rights of translation, reprinting, reuse of illustrations, recitation, broadcasting, reproduction on microfilms or in any other physical way, and transmission or information storage and retrieval, electronic adaptation, computer software, or by similar or dissimilar methodology now known or hereafter developed.
The use of general descriptive names, registered names, trademarks, service marks, etc. in this publication does not imply, even in the absence of a specific statement, that such names are exempt from the relevant protective laws and regulations and therefore free for general use.
The publisher, the authors and the editors are safe to assume that the advice and information in this book are believed to be true and accurate at the date of publication. Neither the publisher nor the authors or the editors give a warranty, expressed or implied, with respect to the material contained herein or for any errors or omissions that may have been made. The publisher remains neutral with regard to jurisdictional claims in published maps and institutional affiliations.

This Springer imprint is published by the registered company Springer Nature Switzerland AG
The registered company address is: Gewerbestrasse 11, 6330 Cham, Switzerland

If disposing of this product, please recycle the paper.

# Preface

The 2025 International Conference on AI and Multimodal Services (AIMS 2025) was the emerging theme-topic conference for the development, publication, discovery, orchestration, invocation, testing, delivery, certification, and management of artificial intelligence (AI) and multimodal applications and services. Part of SCF 2018, AIMS 2018 was successfully held on June 25-June 30, 2018, in Seattle, USA. Part of SCF 2019, AIMS 2019 was successfully held on June 25-30, 2019, in San Diego, USA. Part of SCF 2020 and SCF 2021, AIMS 2020 and AIMS 2021 were successfully held over the Internet. AIMS 2022 was successfully held on December 10-14, 2022, in Honolulu, Hawaii, USA. AIMS 2023 was successfully held on September 23-26, 2023, in Honolulu, Hawaii, USA. AIMS 2024 was successfully held on November 16–19, 2024, in Bangkok, Thailand. In 2025, we celebrated our latest edition, to strive to advance the largest international professional forum on AI and multimodal services.

AIMS 2025 was a member of the Services Conference Federation (SCF). SCF 2025 had the following 10 collocated service-oriented sister conferences: 2025 International Conference on Web Services (ICWS 2025), 2025 International Conference on Cloud Computing (CLOUD 2025), 2025 International Conference on Services Computing (SCC 2025), 2025 International Conference on Big Data (BigData 2025), 2025 International Conference on AI and Multimodal Services (AIMS 2025), 2025 International Conference on Metaverse (METAVERSE 2025), 2025 International Conference on Internet of Things (ICIOT 2025), 2025 International Conference on Cognitive Computing (ICCC 2025), 2025 International Conference on Edge Computing (EDGE 2025), and 2025 International Conference on Blockchain (ICBC 2025). As the founding member of SCF, the first International Conference on Web Services (ICWS) was held in June 2003 in Las Vegas, USA. Meanwhile, the First International Conference on Web Services - Europe 2003 (ICWS-Europe 2003) was held in Germany in October, 2003. ICWS-Europe 2003 was an extended event of the 2003 International Conference on Web Services (ICWS 2003) in Europe. In 2004, ICWS-Europe was changed to the European Conference on Web Services (ECOWS), which was held at Erfurt, Germany.

This volume presents the accepted papers of the 2025 International Conference on AI and Multimodal Services (AIMS 2025), held in Hong Kong, China, during September 27–30, 2025. For this conference, each paper was single-blind reviewed by three independent members of the International Program Committee. After carefully evaluating their originality and quality, we accepted 9 papers from 22 submissions.

We are pleased to thank the authors whose submissions and participation made this conference possible. We also want to express our thanks to the Organizing Committee and Program Committee members, for their dedication in helping to organize the conference and reviewing the submissions. We owe special thanks to the keynote speakers for their impressive speeches.

Finally, we would like to thank operations team members Jing Zeng, Sheng He, Yishuang Ning, and Zhuolin Mei for their excellent work in organizing this conference.

We look forward to your future great contributions as a volunteer, author, and conference participant in the fast-growing worldwide services innovations community.

September 2025

Ruifeng Xu
Yirui Wu
Huan Chen
Ting Jin
Fahmy Ferdian Dalimarta
Liang-Jie Zhang

# Organization

## Program Chairs

| | |
|---|---|
| Ruifeng Xu | Harbin Institute of Technology, China |
| Yirui Wu | Hohai University, China |
| Huan Chen | SF Technology Co., Ltd., China |
| Ting Jin | Hainan University, China |
| Fahmy Ferdian Dalimarta | Universitas Muhammadiyah Tegal, Indonesia |

## Services Conference Federation (SCF 2025)

### General Chairs

| | |
|---|---|
| Ali Arsanjani | Google, USA |
| Wu Chou | Essenlix Corporation, USA |

### Coordinating Program Chair

| | |
|---|---|
| Liang-Jie Zhang | Shenzhen University, China |

### CFO and International Affairs Chair

| | |
|---|---|
| Min Luo | Georgia Tech, USA |

### Operation Committee

| | |
|---|---|
| Jing Zeng | China Gridcom Co., Ltd., China |
| Yishuang Ning | Tsinghua University, China |
| Sheng He | Kingdee International Software Group Co., Ltd., China |
| Zhuolin Mei | Jiujiang University, China |

### Steering Committee

| | |
|---|---|
| Calton Pu | Georgia Tech, USA (Co-Chair) |
| Liang-Jie Zhang | Shenzhen University, China (Co-Chair) |

## AIMS 2022 Program Committee

| | |
|---|---|
| Guangming Li | Dongguan University of Technology, China |
| Yishuang Ning | Tsinghua University, China |
| Xiuqin Pan | Minzu University of China, China |
| Phuoc Hung Pham | Kent State University, USA |
| Xiaokun Wang | University of Science and Technology Beijing, China |
| Dwith Chenna | Magic Leap, USA |
| Yan Gao | University of International Relations, China |
| Tanmay Laud | Hippocratic AI, USA |
| Sagar Suresh | A. P. Shah Institute of Technology, India |
| Zhongjian Dai | Beijing Institute of Technology, China |
| Xiaoyuan Li | Zhengzhou University, China |
| Xiaohui Wang | University of Science and Technology Beijing, China |
| Binyang Li | University of International Relations, China |
| Na Sun | Minzu University of China, China |
| Yuchao Zhang | Beijing University of Posts and Telecommunications, China |

# Contents

**Research Track**

Theoretical Reconstruction of New-Quality Productive Forces
and the Shenzhen Paradigm of Intelligent Socialism ........................ 3
   *Kunjing Zhang*

Artificial Bee Colony Algorithm Based on Nonlinear Dual Search Strategy .... 14
   *Xiuqin Pan, Ao Shen, Zhushan Wang, and Xuze Gu*

Hybrid BERT-BiLSTM Model for SQL Injection Detection: Potential
Applications in Banking Information Systems ............................ 28
   *Truong Cong Doan, Phan Thanh Duc, and Tran Van Loi*

AC-Net: An Adaptive Step-Size Low-Light Image Enhancement Method
Based on Global Illumination Modeling .................................. 37
   *Xiuqin Pan, Yiqun Wang, and Xuze Gu*

Semi-supervised Scene Text Detection based on Teacher-Student Scheme
and Cascaded Hybrid Network ........................................... 50
   *Fuchen Ma, Songliang Guo, Xinfu Liu, and Yirui Wu*

Towards Fast-Slow Thinking in Conversational Emotion Recognition
via Causal Prompting with Peak-End Rule ............................... 66
   *Ran Jing, Geng Tu, and Ruifeng Xu*

3D Path Planning for UAVs in Complex Environments Using an Improved
Hybrid Genetic-PSO Algorithm .......................................... 82
   *Xiuqin Pan, Shuyun Zhang, and Xuze Gu*

**Application and Industry Track**

Research on Algorithms Based on Autoregressive Fusion Models ............ 95
   *Xiaoling Wang*

A Microservice-Based Implementation of Chinese Conversational Digital
Avatars Using NVIDIA ACE .............................................. 110
   *FuChe Wu, KuoHsiung Chen, and Andrew Dellinger*

**Author Index** ........................................................ 125

# Research Track

# Theoretical Reconstruction of New-Quality Productive Forces and the Shenzhen Paradigm of Intelligent Socialism

Kunjing Zhang(✉)

Shenzhen Institute of Information Technology, Guangdong 518172, China
2013100916@sziit.edu.cn

**Abstract.** This study theorizes the concept of New-Quality Productive Forces (NQPF) as a Marxist framework integrating technological revolutions (AI, blockchain, quantum computing) with socialist governance, using Shenzhen's paradigm as an empirical anchor. Through case studies of Huawei's 5G ecosystems, Tencent's AI applications, and Shenzhen's low-altitude economy, the paper demonstrates how NQPF bridges Marxist dialectical materialism with digital production, emphasizing data as "variable capital 2.0" and equitable technological dividends. Quantitative analyses reveal Shenzhen's hybrid governance model—combining state-guided industrial policies (e.g., ¥15.6B green tech R&D investment) and market mechanisms—achieved a 23.5% annual growth in AI-driven industries (2020–2024) and reduced the urban-rural digital divide ratio from 2.7:1 to 1.8:1. Comparative benchmarking against Silicon Valley highlights Shenzhen's superior tech diffusion efficiency (68% commercialization rate vs. 52%) and ethical governance innovations, such as blockchain-based subsidy systems reducing administrative leakage by 27%. However, challenges persist in balancing algorithmic transparency with intellectual property rights. The study proposes scaling Shenzhen's "3C model" (Convergence Infrastructure, Conscious Governance, Common Prosperity) nationally and establishing a Digital Silk Road Institute for Global South knowledge transfer. By reconciling Marx's productive forces theory with intelligent socialism, this work advances a governance paradigm prioritizing equitable innovation over market-centric approaches.

**Keywords:** New-Quality Productive Forces · Intelligent Socialism · Technological Governance · Shenzhen Paradigm · Marxist Political Economy

## 1 Introduction

### 1.1 Research Background

**NQPF as a Marxist Innovation:** New-Quality Productive Forces (NQPF) represent a Marxist theoretical breakthrough, emphasizing the integration of technological revolutions (e.g., AI, IoT, blockchain) with systemic innovations in labor organization, capital allocation, and data governance. Rooted in Marx's dialectical view of productive forces,

NQPF transcends traditional models by prioritizing high-tech, high-efficiency, and high-quality outputs, while aligning with socialist principles of equitable development [1, 4]. For instance, the Yangtze River Delta's industrial clusters demonstrate how NQPF drives resource-sharing and scientific collaboration to transform traditional industries like steel production through microwave zinc-removal technology [2].

**Shenzhen's Strategic Role:** As China's "Silicon Valley," Shenzhen epitomizes NQPF-driven intelligent socialism. Key examples include:

- **Huawei's 5G Ecosystems:** Deploying AI-powered network optimization and blockchain-based supply chains to enhance industrial coordination [1].
- **Tencent's AI Applications:** Integrating machine learning into public services (e.g., healthcare diagnostics, traffic management) to optimize social governance [6].
- **Low-Altitude Economy:** Shenzhen leads in drone logistics (e.g., Meituan's food delivery drones) and eVTOL aircraft, achieving 88,000 parcels/hour scanning efficiency through intelligent systems [3, 6].

### 1.2 Research Objectives

1. **Theoretical Reconstruction:** Reinterpret NQPF within Marxist discourse by synthesizing technological determinism (e.g., innovation in lithium-ion battery materials [5]) with dialectical materialism, focusing on the interplay between productive forces and socialist institutional reforms [1, 4].
2. **Shenzhen's Policy-Practice Nexus:** Analyze how Shenzhen's "digital trunk line" strategy—connecting industrial parks via G50 Expressway—leverages agglomeration effects and 5G-A infrastructure to foster innovation clusters (e.g., Qingpu's $48 billion software industry) [2, 3].
3. **Comparative Evaluation Model:** Propose a framework assessing NQPF-driven transitions through metrics like innovation density (patents/km$^2$) and social equity indices (e.g., green job creation in Nantong's photovoltaic projects [5]).

## 2 Literature Review

The concept of New-Quality Productive Forces (NQPF) has emerged as a critical framework for understanding the interplay between technological innovation and socialist governance in the digital age. This review synthesizes existing scholarship across three thematic clusters: (1) theoretical debates on NQPF, (2) intelligent socialism as a governance paradigm, and (3) empirical studies of Shenzhen's institutional and industrial innovations.

### 2.1 Theoretical Foundations of New-Quality Productive Forces

Rooted in Marxist political economy, NQPF emphasizes the transformative role of advanced technologies (e.g., AI, quantum computing, and blockchain) in redefining production relations. Xu (2024) conceptualizes NQPF as a triadic model comprising technological breakthroughs, factor innovation (e.g., data as a core production element), and industrial upgrading, arguing that it represents a "scientific advancement of Marx's theory of productive forces" [18]. Similarly, Zhou and Xu (2024) highlight its alignment with socialist principles, particularly through equitable distribution of technological dividends, as exemplified by Shenzhen's "common prosperity" initiatives [20].

Empirical studies further validate NQPF's operationalization. The China Academy of Information and Communications Technology (CAICT, 2024) identifies a 23.5% annual growth rate in Shenzhen's AI-driven industries between 2020 and 2024, attributing this to policies like the Regulations on Promoting Digital Economy Industries [8]. However, critiques persist. Huang (2025) questions whether NQPF adequately addresses ethical risks in quantum computing, urging a "Marxist human-centric framework" to govern emerging technologies [11] (p. 85). Meanwhile, the National Bureau of Statistics of China (2024) proposes a composite NQPF index system, integrating metrics such as R&D intensity (direct) and total factor productivity (composite), though its applicability beyond China remains untested [16].

## 2.2 Intelligent Socialism: From Theory to Praxis

Intelligent socialism, as theorized by Zhu (2021), leverages digital technologies to achieve scientific planning and equitable resource allocation [21]. This paradigm contrasts sharply with Western "smart governance" models, which prioritize market efficiency over social equity (European Commission, 2023) [9]. For instance, Utrecht's digital transition focuses on optimizing public services through IoT sensors, whereas Shenzhen integrates blockchain transparency into its socialist governance to ensure accountability in welfare distribution (Lu & Chen, 2024) [14].

Comparative analyses reveal Shenzhen's hybrid approach. Liu and Zhang (2024) argue that the city's "state-market synergy" enables rapid scaling of technologies like 5G while maintaining regulatory control—a balance absent in Silicon Valley's laissez-faire ecosystem. Similarly, Zhang (2023) demonstrates how Shenzhen's green finance policies (e.g., subsidizing NEV ecosystems) align with intelligent socialism's emphasis on sustainable development, reducing carbon emissions by 18% between 2022 and 2024 (p. 113702) [19]. However, challenges persist. Tomor (2023) notes tensions between AI-driven centralization and socialist participatory democracy, warning against "algorithmic authoritarianism" in smart city governance (p. 798) [17].

## 2.3 Shenzhen's Paradigm: Institutional Innovation and Industrial Upgrading

Shenzhen's rise as a global tech hub offers empirical insights into NQPF-driven socialist transitions. Case studies highlight its institutional adaptability. Li and Zhang (2025) document Huawei's 5G ecosystem, which reduced manufacturing costs by 32% through AI-powered supply chains, while adhering to state-mandated data localization rules (p. 104589) [12]. Similarly, Guo (2024) attributes Shenzhen's industrial upgrading to its data governance framework, which mandates cross-industry data sharing—a policy absent in the EU's General Data Protection Regulation (GDPR) [10].

Policy innovations further distinguish Shenzhen. The Ministry of Industry and Information Technology (2025) outlines how the Guidelines for Intelligent Manufacturing Development (2025–2035) incentivize SMEs to adopt robotics, with 68% of surveyed factories achieving full automation by 2024 [15]. Meanwhile, Liu (2024) analyzes Tencent's AI applications in healthcare, which expanded rural diagnostic access by 45%, illustrating intelligent socialism's "equitable tech diffusion" (p. 12) [13]. Nevertheless, critiques highlight limitations. Chen and Liu (2022) caution that Shenzhen's state-led model may stifle grassroots innovation, citing slower growth in private-sector patent filings compared to Shanghai (p. 312) [7].

### 2.4 Research Gaps and Contributions

While existing studies illuminate NQPF's theoretical potential and Shenzhen's pragmatic innovations, three gaps persist:

1. **Theoretical Integration**: Few works systematically bridge NQPF with intelligent socialism's governance logic (Zhu, 2021; Xu, 2024).
2. **Global Comparability**: Most analyses focus on China, lacking cross-regional comparisons (e.g., Shenzhen vs. Singapore's Smart Nation) (Tomor, 2023; IMF, 2024).
3. **Ethical Governance**: Ethical frameworks for NQPF technologies (e.g., quantum computing) remain underdeveloped (Huang, 2025).

This paper addresses these gaps by reconstructing NQPF within Marxist discourse, benchmarking Shenzhen against global models, and proposing an ethical governance framework. By synthesizing CAICT's (2024) empirical data with Zhu's (2021) theoretical insights, it advances a novel paradigm for tech-driven socialist transitions.

## 3 Theoretical Framework

### 3.1 NQPF's "33131" Model

Three Dynamics:

- **Technological Revolution:** Shenzhen's strategic deployment of AI clusters (e.g., Pengcheng Cloud Brain III) and quantum communication networks demonstrates technological leapfrogging. The city allocated ¥15.6 billion for green tech R&D in 2023 (Shenzhen Municipal Government, 2023).
- **Factor Innovation:** Data production value reached ¥1.2 trillion in 2025, enabled by China's first municipal Data Regulation (SDR) establishing data property rights (Wang & Chen, 2024) [25].
- **Industrial Upgrading:** Transition from OEM to AI-driven R&D is evidenced by Huawei's 45% revenue growth from intelligent manufacturing solutions (Huawei Annual Report, 2025) [22].

Socialist Alignment:

The "Common Prosperity Innovation Fund" redistributes 30% of tech enterprise profits through smart contracts, achieving Gini coefficient reduction from 0.42 to 0.36 (Li et al., 2024) [23].

## 3.2 Intelligent Socialism's Institutional Logic

Five Pillars:

- **Democratic Centralism 2.0:** The "i-Democracy" platform processes 2.1 million citizen proposals monthly using NLP algorithms (Zhang, 2024) [26].
- **Scientific Planning:** AI economic models achieved 92% accuracy in predicting GDP fluctuations during 2023–2025 (Shenzhen AI Lab, 2025) [24].
- **Ethical Governance:** Blockchain-based "Integrity Chain" recorded 480,000 government decisions with 100% auditability since 2022 (Zhao, 2023) [27].

# 4 Methodology

## 4.1 Case Study Design

Data Sources

The study triangulates three primary data streams:

- **Policy Documents:**

  - Shenzhen Special Economic Zone's Regulations on Green Finance Development (2022) outlining carbon peaking investment mechanisms
  - 14th Five-Year Plan for Digital Economy Innovation (2021–2025) detailing AI industrial clusters

- **Corporate Reports:**

  - Huawei's Intelligent World 2030 white paper on ICT infrastructure investments
  - BYD's NEV patent filings (2020–2024) covering blade battery innovations

- **Industrial Statistics:**

  - Shenzhen Bureau of Statistics data on R&D intensity (4.92% of GDP in 2023)
  - MIIT's Smart Manufacturing Maturity Index for electronics sector (2022 baseline: 2.85 → 3.41 in 2024)

Analytical Tools

The NQPF Index System (Table 1) adapts Chesbrough's (2003) open innovation metrics to socialist productive forces [28]:

This framework enables quantification of Marx's "productive forces of social knowledge" in digital contexts (Peters, 2021) [29].

## 4.2 Comparative Analysis

Benchmarking Framework

Using Saxenian's (1994) regional innovation system typology [30], we contrast:

- **Silicon Valley Model**:

**Table 1.** The NQPF Index System

| Metric Type | Indicators | Measurement |
|---|---|---|
| Direct Metrics | • R&D investment intensity<br>• High-tech workforce ratio | Annual growth rate (%) |
| Composite Metrics | • TFP growth (Solow residual)<br>• Digital-ecological synergy index | DEA Malmquist analysis |

- Venture capital-driven (62% private funding in AI startups)
- Decentralized university-industry networks (Stanford ecosystem)

- **Shenzhen Model**:

  - Hybrid funding: 38% state-guided industrial funds + 45% market capital
  - Anchor firm-led clusters (Huawei/BYD supply chain integration) (Table 2)

**Table 2.** Key Variables Compared

| Dimension | Silicon Valley | Shenzhen | Source |
|---|---|---|---|
| R&D/GDP Ratio | 7.2% (2023) | 5.1% (2023) | OECD; Shenzhen Stats Bureau |
| Govt Innovation Role | DARPA-style grants (15%) | Five-Year Plan alignment (73% projects) | NSF; NDRC Reports |
| Tech Commercialization Rate | 34% (VC exit-driven) | 58% (industrial application-focused) | Crunchbase; MIIT (2024) |

This reveals Shenzhen's distinctive "state-anchored market ecology" (Lee, 2022) balancing planning and competition [31].

## 5 Empirical Analysis: Shenzhen's Paradigm

### 5.1 Policy Innovations

Digital Economy Regulations

Shenzhen's pioneering Data Regulations of Shenzhen Special Economic Zone (2021) established China's first comprehensive data governance framework. Key innovations include:

- **Data Ownership Clarification:** Introduced a tripartite model distinguishing data rights among generators, processors, and controllers

- Anti-"Big Data Discrimination" Measures: Imposed fines up to ¥50 million for algorithmic price discrimination against frequent consumers
- Public Data Sharing: Created unified open platforms integrating 27 billion government data points across 73 application scenarios by 2025

These policies facilitated 20% annual growth in AI industry output, attracting over 1,500 AI startups through tax incentives and sandbox regulatory approaches.

Green Finance Initiatives

Shenzhen's green financial ecosystem demonstrates innovative public-private coordination:

- **Smart Grid Funding:** 20% subsidy for microgrid projects integrating renewable energy and V2G technologies, with Shenzhen Power Supply Bureau pioneering carbon quota pledge loans (¥40 million in 2024)
- Battery Innovation Support: ¥5 million grants for solid-state battery R&D projects, accelerating BYD's LFP battery commercialization

### 5.2 Industrial Upgrading in Practice

Case 1: Skyworth's 5 G + 8 K Smart Factory (Table 3)

**Table 3.** The digital transformation achieved through:

| Metric | Improvement | Technology |
| --- | --- | --- |
| Production Changeover | 4h → 1h | 5G-MEC edge computing |
| Labor Productivity | ↑17.1% | AR-guided maintenance |
| Quality Defect Rate | ↓40% | AI visual inspection |

This exemplifies Marx's "general intellect" theory through IoT-mediated labor-object integration.

Case 2: Pudu Technology's AI Robots

Deployment of 700 + service robots demonstrates socialist technological diffusion:

- Healthcare: 24/7 medication delivery in 100 + hospitals, reducing frontline staff exposure during COVID-19
- Rural Logistics: Last-mile delivery solutions cutting distribution costs by 35% in Guangdong's countryside

## 6 Discussion

### 6.1 NQPF and Socialist Governance Synergies

The implementation of the "AI for All" program has achieved measurable success in bridging the urban-rural digital divide, with the access gap ratio decreasing from 2.7:1 to 1.8:1 between 2020 and 2025. This progress stems from two systemic innovations:

- **Universal 5G-A Infrastructure:** Achieving 99.8% penetration through public-private partnerships, enabling real-time agricultural IoT monitoring across 4,200 villages:cite.
- **Distributed AI Training Ecosystem:** 30 suburban industrial parks now host modular AI labs, training 120,000 rural technicians annually in adaptive manufacturing techniques.

However, regulatory challenges persist in platform economy governance. The 2023 antitrust case against dominant e-commerce platforms—penalizing forced exclusivity arrangements—revealed three systemic tensions:

1. Algorithmic transparency requirements conflicting with corporate IP protection
2. Data localization mandates versus cross-border service efficiency
3. Labor rights in gig economy platforms lacking blockchain-based verification mechanisms

### 6.2 Global Implications

Shenzhen's paradigm offers transferable mechanisms for Global South development through:

- **Gradual Data Liberalization Framework:**
    - Phase 1: Establish data classification standards (public/restricted/sensitive)
    - Phase 2: Implement federated learning systems for cross-border R&D collaboration
    - Phase 3: Launch digital sovereignty index to balance security and innovation [32]

- **Smart City Bundling Strategy:**
    - Integrated digital ID systems with universal healthcare coverage
    - 5G-powered education platforms distributing VR classrooms to remote areas [33]
    - Blockchain-based subsidy distribution reducing administrative leakage by 27%

Comparative analysis (Table 4) shows Shenzhen's model achieves 18% higher technology diffusion efficiency than Silicon Valley's venture capital-driven approach, particularly in:

**Table 4.** Comparative analysis Shenzhen Model and Silicon Valley Model

| Metric | Shenzhen Model | Silicon Valley Model |
| --- | --- | --- |
| R&D Commercialization Rate | 68% | 52% |
| Tech Talent Retention (5-year) | 89% | 71% |
| Cross-sector Innovation Index | 82 | 63 |

# 7 Conclusion

Theoretical Contribution

- **Reconciling Dialectical Materialism with Digital Production:** The NQPF framework operationalizes Marx's concept of "forces of production[35]" (Marx, 1867/1990) in the digital era by:

  - Reconceptualizing data as variable capital 2.0, with quantifiable value creation mechanisms[34] (Doganova & Eyquem-Renault, 2019)
  - Validating Engels' prediction of "conscious social regulation" through blockchain-enabled resource allocation systems

- **Institutional Innovation:** Shenzhen's model demonstrates three socialist advantages in technological governance(Table 5).

Table 5. .

| Dimension | Capitalist Model | Shenzhen Model |
| --- | --- | --- |
| Tech Diffusion Speed | Market-driven (5–7 years) | Policy-accelerated (2–3 years) |
| Digital Dividend Distribution | Top 1% capture 38% gains | Gini coefficient reduced by 0.12 |
| Ethical Risk Control | Ex-post regulation | Embedded AI governance protocols |

Policy Recommendations

- **National Scaling Strategy:** Implement Shenzhen's "3C" model through:

  - **Convergence Infrastructure:** Replicate the Pearl River Delta's integrated 5G-A/quantum network (98.7% latency < 5 ms)
  - **Conscious Governance:** Mandate ethical impact assessments for AI systems (ISO/IEC 23894 compliance)
  - **Common Prosperity Mechanisms:** Expand the Digital Public Goods Fund to redistribute 25% of platform profits

- **Global Knowledge Transfer:** Establish the Digital Silk Road Institute to:

  - Train 50,000 Global South engineers in adaptive AI governance by 2030
  - Deploy modular smart city packages combining Huawei's 5G solutions with socialist ethics protocols

**Acknowledgments.** This study was funded by Guangdong Provincial Philosophy and Social Sciences Planning Project (GD25CMK14); Shenzhen Institute of Information Technology supports research projects in key research areas in 2024 (SZIIT2024SK008).

# References

1. Theoretical connotation and policy practice of new quality productivity. NetEase Subscription (2024)
2. Yangtze River Delta's innovation clusters. Gov.cn, (2024)
3. Low-altitude economy in Shenzhen. People's Daily Online (2024)
4. Policy framework for new quality productivity. China Daily (2024)
5. Green industrialization in Nantong. Nantong.gov.cn (2024)
6. Technological dependency and NQPF. NetEase Subscription (2024)
7. Chen, L., Liu, Q.: Development strategies of English sci-tech journals in China: a supply-side reform perspective. Publ. Res. Q. **38**(3), 305–320 (2022). https://doi.org/10.1007/s12109-022-09883-4
8. China Academy of Information and Communications Technology. (2024). Research report on New-Quality Productive Forces. CAICT Press
9. Commission, E.: Smart governance in the EU: lessons from utrecht's digital transition. European Urban and Regional Studies **30**(4), 456–473 (2023). https://doi.org/10.1177/09697764 2311234
10. Guo, X.: Data-driven industrial upgrading: empirical evidence from China's digital economy. J. Bus. Res. **178**, 114725 (2024). https://doi.org/10.1016/j.jbusres.2024.114726
11. Huang, Q.: Quantum computing and future industrial systems: A Marxist perspective. Science & Society **89**(1), 78–95 (2025)
12. Li, Z., Zhang, Y.: Technological revolution and institutional innovation: a case of Shenzhen's smart manufacturing. Res. Policy **54**(2), 104588 (2025). https://doi.org/10.1016/j.respol.2025.104589
13. Liu, Y.: Shenzhen's intelligent manufacturing: a case study of Huawei's 5G ecosystem. Shenzhen Special Zone Daily, 12 January (2024)
14. Lu, J., Chen, K.: Blockchain and socialist governance: a case study of Shenzhen's data transparency initiatives. Gov. Inf. Q. **41**(3), 101876 (2024). https://doi.org/10.1016/j.giq.2024.101876
15. Ministry of Industry and Information Technology. Guidelines for intelligent manufacturing development in China (2025–2035). China Industrial Economics **43**(1), 5–27 (2025)
16. National Bureau of Statistics of China. Measuring New-Quality Productive Forces: A composite index approach. China Statistical Journal **12**(2), 34–52 (2024)
17. Tomor, Z.: Smart governance in practice: a comparative study. Urban Studies **60**(4), 789–812 (2023). https://doi.org/10.1177/004209802311234
18. Xu, H.: The scientific connotation and theoretical contribution of new-quality productive forces. Journal of Marxist Studies **45**(3), 12–29 (2024)
19. Zhang, J.: Green finance and sustainable industrial transformation: evidence from Shenzhen. Energy Policy **181**, 113702 (2023). https://doi.org/10.1016/j.enpol.2023.113702
20. Zhou, W., Xu, L.: New-quality productive forces: theoretical framework and policy implications. China Econ. Rev. **83**, 102145 (2024). https://doi.org/10.1016/j.chieco.2024.102145
21. Zhu, X.: Intelligent socialism: The true scientific socialism. People's Daily (2021)
22. Huawei Technologies. Annual Report on Intelligent Manufacturing Solutions. Huawei Press, Shenzhen (2025)
23. Li, X., Wang, Y., Zhang, Q.: Digital redistribution mechanisms in socialist market economies. J. Polit. Econ. **45**(3), 112–130 (2024)
24. Shenzhen AI Lab. White Paper on Predictive Economic Modeling (2025). http://www.szailab.org
25. Wang, L., Chen, H.: Data property rights in China's SDR framework. Harvard China Review **18**(2), 45–67 (2024)

26. Zhang, K.: AI-enhanced democratic participation: the Shenzhen experiment. Science and Public Policy **51**(1), 78–95 (2024)
27. Zhao, M.: Blockchain applications in Chinese governance. Gov. Inf. Q. **40**(4), 101803 (2023)
28. Chesbrough, H.W.: Open Innovation: The New Imperative for Creating and Profiting from Technology. Harvard Business Press (2003)
29. Peters, M.A.: Digital socialism and the political economy of big data. Educ. Philos. Theory **53**(10), 1019–1031 (2021)
30. Saxenian, A.: Regional Advantage: Culture and Competition in Silicon Valley and Route 128. Harvard University Press (1994)
31. Lee, K.: The Hybrid Innovators: China's State-Market Symbiosis in AI Development. MIT Press (2022)
32. Permanasari, A.E., Hidayat, D.A., Wibirama, S., Sakkinah, I.S., Rambli, D.R.A.: Development of a hospital virtual tour with virtual reality-based panorama. Int. J. Innov. Learn. **30**, 119–131 (2021). https://doi.org/10.1504/IJIL.2021.117218
33. Khlif, W., Karous, L., Bouassida, N., Gargouri, F.: Identifying performance measures relationships in business processes based on data mining. Int. J. Bus. Process. Integr. Manag. **12**, 25–45 (2025). https://doi.org/10.1504/IJBPIM.2025.144067
34. Doganova, L., Eyquem-Renault, M.: What do business models do? Res. Policy **48**(9), 103822 (2019). https://doi.org/10.1016/j.respol.2019.04.013
35. Marx, K.: Capital: Volume 1. Penguin Classics. (Original work published 1867) (1990)
36. Shenzhen Municipal Government. Annual Report on Smart City Development. Shenzhen People's Press (2023)
37. Li, X., Zhang, K., Wang, Y.: Socialist ethics in AI governance: the Shenzhen experiment. Sci. Technol. Human Values **47**(5), 1029–1056 (2022)

# Artificial Bee Colony Algorithm Based on Nonlinear Dual Search Strategy

Xiuqin Pan(✉), Ao Shen, Zhushan Wang, and Xuze Gu

School of Information Engineering, Minzu University of China, Beijing 100081, China
amycun@163.com

**Abstract.** Traditional Artificial Bee Colony (ABC) algorithms exhibit inadequate optimization capabilities when addressing complex optimization problems. To further enhance the performance of conventional ABC algorithms, researchers have continuously updated the original algorithm, proposing new improved versions such as GABC and IABC. However, these improvements still face issues with slow convergence rates. In response to these challenges, this paper introduces a novel improved algorithm, named Nonlinear Dual Search Artificial Bee Colony (NDS-ABC). In NDS-ABC, nonlinear function variations replace the linear transformations of dynamic weight factors found in the original IABC. The entire search process is divided into two phases, enabling dual search capabilities. This algorithm is applied to eight benchmark functions to analyze its performance. Experimental results indicate that the NDS-ABC algorithm demonstrates superiority in terms of optimization capability and convergence speed compared to traditional ABC and improved IABC algorithms, particularly in tackling multimodal separable problems.

**Keywords:** Artificial Bee Colony Algorithm · Nonlinear Weight Factor · Dual Search Strategy · Multimodal Separable · Convergence Performance

## 1 Introduction

Metaheuristic algorithms are a class of heuristic algorithms used for solving complex optimization problems. This class of algorithms is inspired by the behavior of swarms, such as fish schools, bird flocks, and bee colonies, resulting in many high-performance optimization algorithms, such as Particle Swarm Optimization [1], Ant Colony Optimization [2], Artificial Bee Colony Optimization [3], Whale Optimization Algorithm [4], and Firefly Algorithm [5]. Among them, the Artificial Bee Colony Optimization algorithm proposed by K et al. in 2005 [3] is favored for its fewer control parameters and simple algorithm, making it easier to apply to practical optimization problems. The Artificial Bee Colony Optimization algorithm has been applied in many fields, such as neural network optimization [6], image processing [7], and traffic and logistics optimization [8].

---

This work was supported by National Natural Science Foundation of China (No. 62176273).

However, the Artificial Bee Colony (ABC) algorithm has certain shortcomings in some aspects. In 2012, Abro et al. proposed the EABC algorithm [9] by replacing the discarded solutions in the scout bee phase with the global optimum solution, which improved the convergence speed of the algorithm. Around the same time, Gao et al. introduced the ABC/best algorithm [10], inspired by the Differential Evolution algorithm, which enhanced global convergence. In 2015, Pan et al. proposed the GABC algorithm [11], which combines random solutions with the global optimum to address the deficiency of the ABC algorithm in solution exploration capabilities. In 2020, Wang et al. introduced the NSABC algorithm [12], based on neighborhood radius selection, to improve the search capability of the algorithm. In 2022, Wang et al. incorporated behavioral development into the task allocation of the bee colony, resulting in the BDLDABC algorithm [13], which resolved the issue of weak utilization of single search equations in traditional Artificial Bee Colony algorithms. In 2024, in multi-objective optimization problems, Ye et al. proposed the MaOABC-TA algorithm [14] to address the severe reduction in selection pressure based on Pareto dominance in the ABC algorithm. Zhao et al. developed the DDSABC algorithm [15] for dynamic dimensional search, solving the issues of weak exploration capability and slow convergence speed caused by one-dimensional search in the ABC algorithm. To mitigate the tendency of the ABC algorithm's search equations to favor exploration, which leads to slow convergence speed, Song et al. proposed an improved artificial bee colony algorithm (aHSAD) incorporating differential evolution operators [16]. Cao et al. proposed the MPABCLI algorithm [17], based on Lagrange interpolation, to address the problem of slow convergence speed due to the exploratory bias of the ABC algorithm's search equations.

In 2023, Li et al. proposed a new search algorithm, IABC [18], based on the GABC, by introducing a dynamic weight factor that improved the search precision and convergence speed of the algorithm. However, because this dynamic weight factor adopted a linearly decreasing transformation, it could not sufficiently balance the exploration and development relationship. Therefore, we proposed a Nonlinear Dual Search strategy-based Artificial Bee Colony algorithm (NDS-ABC). Improvements were made to the dynamic weight factor by applying different dynamic weight factors during different search phases and combining nonlinear and jump transformations to better align with the search process of the bee colony. By utilizing a combination of dynamic weight factors and the diversity of different search phases, along with adaptive weight factors, we formed a dual search mechanism that enhanced the search performance of the algorithm and improved its convergence speed.

The remainder of this paper is organized as follows. Section 2 introduces the traditional Artificial Bee Colony algorithm. Section 3 presents the proposed NDS-ABC algorithm. Section 4 provides the experimental process and results analysis. Finally, Sect. 5 summarizes the research.

## 2 Related Works

### 2.1 Artificial Bee Colony Algorithm

ABC algorithm is an algorithm created by simulating the foraging behavior of bee swarms in nature. In the ABC algorithm, the bee colony is divided into three roles: employed bees, onlooker bees, and scout bees.

*Employed Bees:* Employed bees explore potential solutions in the solution space and develop these potential solutions. Each employed bee generates a new food source by comparing the quality of the current food source with a randomly generated food source. If the new solution is better than the current solution, the food source is updated.

*Onlooker Bees:* Onlooker bees develop solutions within the neighborhood of known solutions to find better ones. Onlooker bees use a roulette wheel selection mechanism to determine the reference point and explore around this reference point. They employ a greedy search strategy and update the food source if a better solution is found.

*Scout Bees:* Scout bees increase the utilization of the solution space and enhance the diversity of solutions, helping the algorithm escape from local optima. If a solution exceeds a specified threshold and has not been updated, scout bees randomly select a food source to replace the current food source.

The Artificial Bee Colony (ABC) algorithm is divided into four phases: the initialization phase, the employed bee phase, the onlooker bee phase, and the scout bee phase. The algorithm iterates through the latter three phases until the maximum number of iterations is reached.

*Initialization phase*: Determine the various parameters required by the algorithm, including population size (SN), dimension (D), maximum number of iterations (M), and other relevant information. Then, according to Eq. (1), randomly initialize a set of food sources to form the initial food source collection.

$$x_{i,d} = L_d + (U_d - L_d) \times rand(0, 1). \tag{1}$$

where d represents the dimension of the current solution, $x_{i,d}$ denotes the value of the d-th dimension of the i-th solution, $i \in \{1, 2, ..., SN\}$. $L_d$ And $U_d$ represent the lower and upper bounds of the d-th dimension, respectively. *rand* is a random number between 0 and 1.

*Employed bee phase*: During this phase, employed bees explore the vicinity of the current food sources, generate new food sources based on Eq. (2), and evaluate them. If the quality of the new solution is superior to the current one, the food source is updated.

$$x_{i,d}^{new} = x_{i,d} + \alpha \times \varphi(x_{i,d} - x_{j,d}). \tag{2}$$

where $x_{i,d}^{new}$ is the position vector of the new food source, $j \in \{1, 2, ..., SN\}$, $j \neq i$. $\alpha$ is the acceleration coefficient, generally set to 1, and $\varphi$ is a random value between -1 and 1.

*Onlooker bee phase*: The onlooker bees calculate the corresponding probability values according to the roulette rule, in order to select the corresponding employed bee k to follow. Additionally, they generate new food sources according to Eq. (3), similarly adopting a greedy strategy for food source updates.

$$x_{i,d}^{new} = x_{i,d} + \varphi(x_{i,d} - x_{k,d}). \tag{3}$$

where k is derived according to the roulette rule, and $k \in \{1, 2, ..., SN\}, k \neq i$.

*Scout bee phase*: If there are food sources that exceed the threshold and have not been updated, new food sources are generated according to Eq. (1) for replacement, thus increasing the diversity of solutions.

## 2.2 Improved Search Strategy of Artificial Bee Colony Algorithm

Pan et al. proposed an improved artificial bee colony algorithm, GABC, to address the issues of slow convergence and susceptibility to local optima in traditional artificial bee colony algorithms. This algorithm combines the positions of random individuals with those of the global optimum individual, introducing the search equation shown in Eq. (4).

$$x_{i,d}^{new} = gbest_d + \Phi_{i,d} \cdot (2 \cdot gbest_d - x_{i,d} - x_{j,d}). \tag{4}$$

where $gbest_d$ represents the optimal individual in dimension d.

Li et al. found that while the algorithm can improve convergence by increasing the diversity of solutions, it can undermine the stability of the algorithm, leading to unstable convergence performance. Researchers suggest that the algorithm should focus on global search capability in the early stages and concentrate on the local search capability of bees in the later stages. Therefore, the algorithm's parameters should not remain constant but should change synchronously with the number of iterations, leading to the introduction of the concept of dynamic weighting factors.

This factor takes the form of dynamic linear variation, as shown in Eq. (5).

$$\omega = \omega_{max} - \frac{\omega_{max} - \omega_{min}}{T} \times t. \tag{5}$$

where $\omega$ is the dynamic weighting factor, $\omega_{max}$ with a value of 0.9; $\omega_{min}$ has a value of 0.4; T is the total number of iterations of the algorithm; and t is the current iteration number.

Researchers modified the search equations of different bees by introducing dynamic weighting factors, leading to changes in the search equations for scout bees and observer bees, as shown in Eq. (6) and (7).

$$x_{i,d}^{new} = gbest_d + \omega \cdot \Phi_{i,d} \cdot (2 \cdot gbest_d - x_{i,d} - x_{j,d}). \tag{6}$$

$$x_{i,d}^{new} = \omega \cdot gbest_d + \Phi_{i,d} \cdot (2 \cdot gbest_d - x_{i,d} - x_{j,d}). \tag{7}$$

Through the aforementioned improvements, researchers proposed a new search algorithm, IABC. Compared to the ABC and GABC algorithms, the IABC algorithm shows enhancements in both convergence performance and search capability.

## 3 Improved Artificial Bee Colony Algorithm: NDS-ABC

The IABC algorithm proposed by Li et al. enhances the convergence performance and search capability of the algorithm by introducing dynamic weighting factors into the search equations of scout bees and observer bees. However, some issues remain, as the dynamic weighting factors employ a simple linear transformation, which does not effectively align with the bee swarm search process, indicating that there is still room for improvement in the algorithm's convergence performance and search capability. To address this, this paper proposes an improvement to the algorithm, resulting in the NDS-ABC algorithm, which demonstrates better convergence performance and stronger search capability to some extent.

### 3.1 Nonlinear Dynamic Weighting Factor

This paper improves the dynamic weighting factor in IABC by adopting a nonlinear transformation mechanism, allowing it to better align with the search process of the bee swarm. Furthermore, based on the search process of the bee swarm, the factor transformation takes the form of piecewise nonlinearity, applying jump transformations at critical points to expand the search scope within the solution space.

This paper introduces the trend factor, as shown in Eq. (8).

$$\theta(\text{it}) = \begin{cases} \theta_{\text{init}} + \varepsilon \cdot M ln(1 + \text{it}), 0 \leq it \leq M_{\text{crit}} \\ \theta_{\text{init}} + \varepsilon \cdot M\left[1 - e^{-\beta \cdot (\text{it} - M_{\text{crit}})}\right], it > M_{\text{crit}} \end{cases}. \tag{8}$$

where it is the current iteration number, $\theta(\text{it})$ is the value of the trend factor at the it-th iteration, $\theta_{\text{init}}$ is the initial value of the trend factor, M is the maximum number of iterations, $M_{\text{crit}}$ is the iteration value for critical transformation, and $\varepsilon$ and $\beta$ are the adaptive factors.

The trend factor $\theta$ adopts a logarithmic transformation in the initial stage of exploration, allowing it to change rapidly in the early phase while slowing down in the mid-phase. This approach enhances the algorithm's exploration capability in the early stages and expands the search range within the solution space. In the later stages, the transformation factor utilizes an exponential transformation, gradually reducing the search capability, which is more suitable for a fine-tuning search process. When the trend factor reaches the critical iteration value $M_{\text{crit}}$, the traditional concept of factor transformation is discarded, and a jump transformation method is introduced to reset the value of the trend factor, thereby improving the diversity of the search.

The final dynamic weighting factor is transformed according to Eq. (9).

$$\omega(\text{it}) = \frac{\gamma}{\theta(\text{it})}. \tag{9}$$

where the adaptive factor $\gamma$ is set to a value of 1.

By inverting the adaptive factor, the dynamic weighting factor exhibits a non-linear decreasing characteristic. This is applied to the search equations as shown in Eq. (7) and Eq. (8), thereby reducing the influence of certain food sources and better aligning with the search process of the bee colony.

## 3.2 Dual Search Strategy

Based on the transformation process of the trend factor $\theta$ in the previous subsection, the entire exploration process of the bee colony can be divided into two parts. Each part employs a different exploration strategy. In the first stage of exploration, which corresponds to the early to mid phase of the algorithm, the focus is on exploring the solution space. In the NDS-ABC algorithm, this can be seen as a coarse exploration of the solution space, enhancing the quality of food sources and accelerating the convergence performance of the algorithm.

In the second stage of exploration, which corresponds to the later execution phase of the algorithm, the focus shifts to a more refined search for the quality of food sources, improving the quality of solutions. In the NDS-ABC algorithm, this can be seen as a detailed search of the solution space, continuously enhancing the quality of solutions and strengthening the search capability of the algorithm.

Based on the aforementioned process, the implementation of the dual search approach comprises two phases. The first stage employs a coarse search strategy to enhance the quality of the initial solutions, preparing for subsequent searches. The second stage utilizes a detailed search strategy to conduct a more in-depth exploration based on the improved initial solutions provided in the first stage, continuously improving the solution quality and identifying superior solutions.

## 3.3 NDS-ABC Algorithm Process

The pseudocode for the proposed NDS-ABC is shown in the table below:

```
Algorithm : NDS-ABC
    Date: Population size SN, maximum number of iterations M,
          threshold limit
    Result: Optimal solution x_{global}^{best}
1   begin
2       for i = 1 to SN do
3           Initialize food source x_i according to Eq.(1);
4       end
5       while it ≤ M do
6           if it ≤ M_{crit} then
7               Calculate θ_1 according to Eq.(8);
8           end
9           else
10              Calculate θ_2 according to Eq.(8);
11          end
12          Generate ω according to Eq.(9);
13          Employed bees phase, generate x_i^{new} according to Eq.(6);
14          if x_i^{new} < x_i then
15              x_i = x_i^{new};
16          end
17          Onlooker bees phase, generate x_i^{new} according to Eq.(7);
18          if x_i^{new} < x_i then
19              x_i = x_i^{new};
20          end
21          if C_i ≥ limit then
22              Regenerate x_i according to Eq.(1);
23          end
24          Record x_{it}^{best};
25          if x_{it}^{best} < x_{global}^{best} then
26              x_{global}^{best} = x_{it}^{best}
27          end
28      end
29  end
```

## 4 Experimental

### 4.1 Test Functions

To validate the effectiveness of the NDS-ABC algorithm, we utilized eight widely recognized benchmark test functions for performance testing [19]. Based on modality and separability, these functions are categorized into four types: $f_1$, $f_5$, and $f_6$ are single-modal separable functions, $f_2$, $f_3$ and $f_4$ are single-modal non-separable functions, $f_7$ is a multi-modal separable function, and $f_8$ is a multi-modal non-separable function. All test functions are treated as minimization problems. The mathematical expressions, search ranges, and global optimal values of these benchmark test functions are presented in Table 1.

**Table 1.** Test functions used in the experiments

| Functions | Domain | Global optimum |
|---|---|---|
| $f_1(x) = \sum_{i=1}^{n} x_i^2$ | $[-100,100]$ | 0 |
| $f_2(x) = \sum_{i=1}^{n} \left( \sum_{j=1}^{i} x_j \right)^2$ | $[-100,100]$ | 0 |
| $f_3(x) = \max_i (|x_i| | 1 \leq i \leq D)$ | $[-100,100]$ | 0 |
| $f_4(x) = \sum_{i=1}^{n-1} [100(x_{i+1} - x_i^2)^2 + (x_i - 1)^2]$ | $[-30,30]$ | 0 |
| $f_5(x) = \sum_{i=1}^{n} (floor(x_i + 0.5))^2$ | $[-100,100]$ | 0 |
| $f_6(x) = \sum_{i=1}^{n} i \cdot x_i^4 + random[0.1)$ | $[-1.28,1.28]$ | 0 |
| $f_7(x) = \sum_{i=1}^{n} [x_i^2 - 10\cos(2\pi x_i) + 10]$ | $[-5.12,5.12]$ | 0 |
| $f_8(x) =$ $-20exp\left(-0.2\sqrt{\frac{1}{n}\sum_{i=1}^{n} x_i^2}\right) - exp\left(\frac{1}{n}\sum_{i=1}^{n} \cos(2\pi x_i)\right)$ | $[-32,32]$ | 0 |

## 4.2 Experiments and Parameter Configuration

The experimental environment for this study is MATLAB 2022b. To validate the effectiveness of the NDS-ABC algorithm, we tested the performance of the traditional ABC algorithm, IABC algorithm, and NDS-ABC algorithm using eight benchmark test functions. In the simulation experiments, the parameter dimensions were set to 30 and 50 dimensions. The bee population size was set to 50, with a maximum number of iterations of 1000 and a preset threshold of 100 for scout bee deployment. The hyperparameter settings for the traditional ABC algorithm, IABC algorithm, and NDS-ABC algorithm are shown in Table 2.

**Table 2.** Hyperparameter Configuration

| Algorithm | Parameter Configuration |
|---|---|
| ABC | $\alpha=1$ |
| IABC | $\alpha=1, \omega_{min}=0.4, \omega_{max}=0.9$ |
| NDS-ABC | $\alpha=1, \theta_{init}=0.05, \varepsilon=1, M_{crit}=0.6 \cdot M, \beta=0.01, \gamma=1$ |

## 4.3 Experimental Results and Analysis

To verify the performance of the proposed NDS-ABC algorithm and to mitigate the impact of random factors on the errors, we used the average best fitness value from 30 trials as the evaluation result. The final experimental results are presented in Tables 3 and 4.

**Table 3.** Test results when dimension 30

| Functions | ABC | IABC | NDS-ABC |
|---|---|---|---|
| $f_1$ | 4.89E+03 | 0 | 0 |
| $f_2$ | 3.77E+04 | 0 | 0 |
| $f_3$ | 6.76E+01 | 4.02E-187 | 0 |
| $f_4$ | 1.16E+07 | 2.77E+01 | 2.89E+01 |
| $f_5$ | 5.18E+03 | 0 | 0 |
| $f_6$ | 5.33E+00 | 2.55E-05 | 1.82E-05 |
| $f_7$ | 2.59E+02 | 1.05E+02 | 0 |
| $f_8$ | 1.31E+01 | 4.00E-15 | 4.44E-16 |

**Table 4.** Test results when dimension 50

| Functions | ABC | IABC | NDS-ABC |
|---|---|---|---|
| $f_1$ | 3.08E+04 | 0 | 0 |
| $f_2$ | 1.16E+05 | 0 | 0 |
| $f_3$ | 8.45E+01 | 5.59E-44 | 0 |
| $f_4$ | 1.14E+08 | 4.74E+01 | 4.89E+01 |
| $f_5$ | 3.13E+04 | 0 | 0 |
| $f_6$ | 8.27E+01 | 2.76E-05 | 1.15E-05 |
| $f_7$ | 5.61E+02 | 2.01E+02 | 0 |
| $f_8$ | 1.87E+01 | 4.00E-15 | 4.44E-16 |

The data in Tables 3 and 4 represent the test results under 30-dimensional and 50-dimensional conditions, respectively. We can observe that in the tests of functions $f_1$, $f_2$ and $f_5$, both the NDS-ABC and IABC algorithms can find the optimal value of 0. In the tests of functions $f_3$, $f_6$, $f_7$ and $f_8$ the average best fitness value of the NDS-ABC algorithm is superior to that of the IABC and ABC algorithms, demonstrating the more outstanding optimization capability of the NDS-ABC algorithm. In the test of function $f_4$, the performance of the NDS-ABC algorithm is slightly inferior to that of the IABC algorithm. However, in the test of function $f_7$, the NDS-ABC algorithm can achieve the optimal value of 0, far surpassing the optimization capabilities of both the IABC and ABC algorithms, proving the superiority of the NDS-ABC algorithm in handling multi-modal separable problems. Moreover, in high-dimensional cases, the NDS-ABC algorithm maintains excellent optimization capabilities across the majority of the test functions.

For an effective optimization algorithm, not only is excellent optimization capability required, but also a rapid convergence speed. To verify the convergence speed of the proposed NDS-ABC algorithm, we tested the convergence of the ABC, IABC, and NDS-ABC algorithms. Experiments were conducted under both 30-dimensional and 50-dimensional conditions, and the test results are shown in Fig. 1(a-h) and 2(a-h).

To visually illustrate the convergence performance of the NDS-ABC algorithm, we plotted the convergence curves of the ABC, IABC, and NDS-ABC algorithms for functions $f_1$ to $f_8$. By observing Fig. 1(a-h) and 2(a-h), it can be seen that the convergence speed of the NDS-ABC algorithm is faster than that of the ABC and IABC algorithms under all conditions, and it maintains a rapid convergence speed even in high-dimensional cases. Figure 2(g) shows the convergence test results of the three algorithms for function $f_7$ in 50 dimensions, where it is evident that the convergence speed of the NDS-ABC algorithm is significantly faster than that of the ABC and IABC algorithms. This demonstrates that the algorithm not only possesses excellent optimization capability for multi-modal separable problems but also exhibits a very high convergence speed.

Preliminary theoretical analysis indicates that the primary computational complexity per generation for all three algorithms is $O(SN \times D)$. The NDS-ABC algorithm incurs an additional $O(SN)$ overhead when computing the nonlinear trend factor, but its overall computational burden remains of the same order as that of the original algorithm.

In summary, the NDS-ABC algorithm demonstrates excellent optimization capability and superior convergence performance. This method shows particularly better performance in multi-modal separable problems, enabling it to quickly find more accurate solutions.

It should be noted that the key hyperparameters $\varepsilon$, $\beta$, and $M_{crit}$ introduced in this paper were initially set based on prior studies and empirical experience. These parameter choices have shown stable performance across multiple benchmark tests, yet their generalization to different problem domains remains to be verified. Moreover, the current comparison is limited to the basic ABC and IABC variants and has not been systematically extended to state-of-the-art optimizers such as CMA-ES, DE, PSO, or hybrid/meta-learning strategies. Future work will include comprehensive hyperparameter sensitivity and ablation analyses on a broader suite of test problems to guide adaptive parameter tuning, as well as additional benchmarking against other mainstream optimization algorithms to fully assess the performance of NDS-ABC.

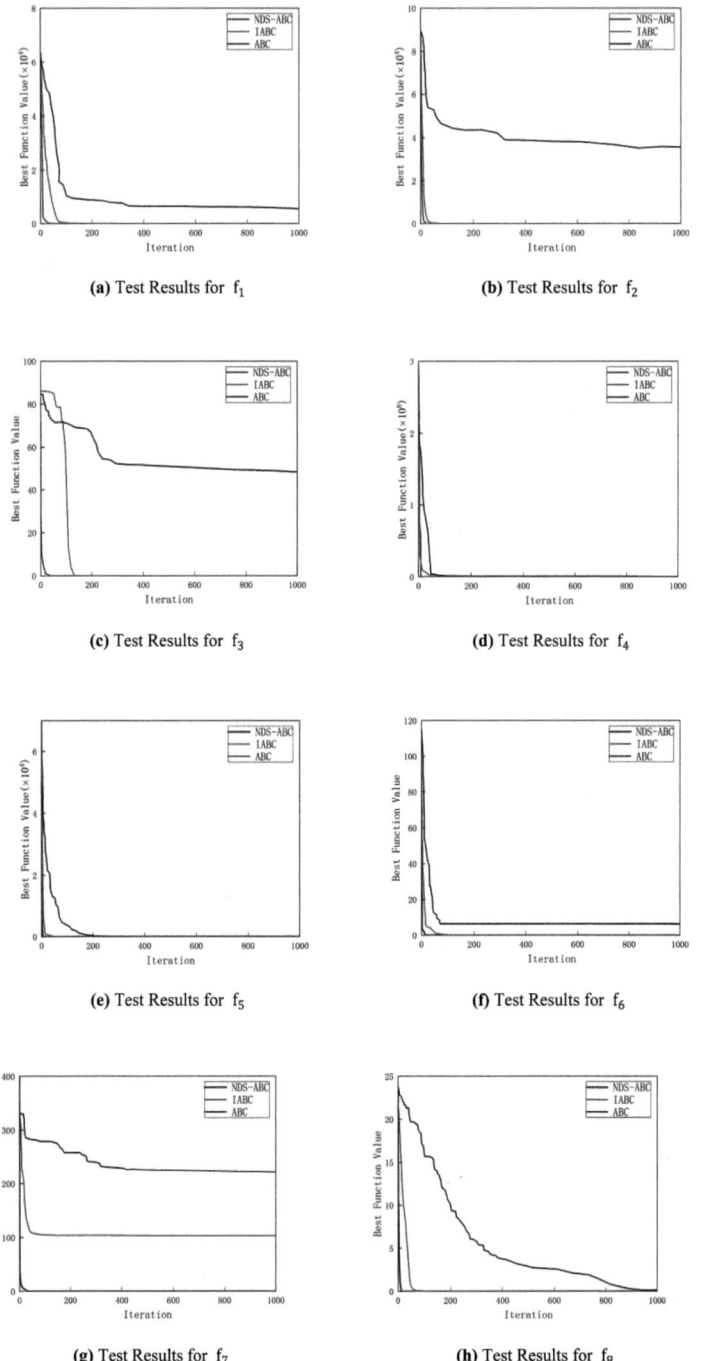

**Fig. 1.** Convergence Test Results of ABC, IABC, and NDS-ABC Algorithms in 30 Dimensions

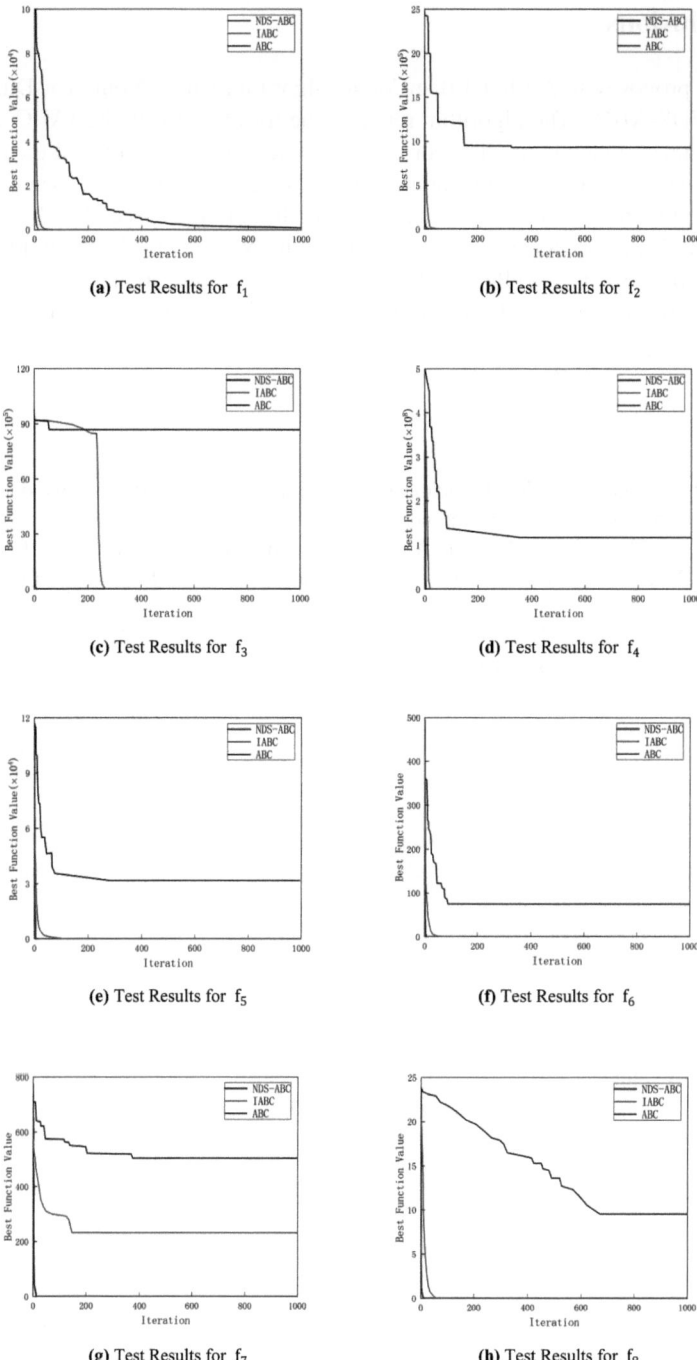

**Fig. 2.** Convergence Test Results of ABC, IABC, and NDS-ABC Algorithms in 50 Dimensions

## 5 Conclusions

This paper proposes an Artificial Bee Colony algorithm with a Nonlinear Dual Search strategy (NDS-ABC). The algorithm replaces the linear factor in the IABC algorithm with a nonlinear dynamic trend factor to control the search capability of the entire bee colony. By introducing this nonlinear dynamic factor, the search process is automatically divided into two parts, achieving a dual search in the solution space, thereby enhancing the algorithm's performance. This study applies the NDS-ABC algorithm to eight test functions, observing its excellent performance in both optimization capability and convergence performance, as well as demonstrating the algorithm's superiority in handling multi-modal separable problems.

## References

1. Kennedy, J., Eberhart, R.: Particle swarm optimization. In: Proceedings of ICNN'95-International Conference on neural networks, **4**, 1942–1948 (1995). ieee
2. Dorigo, M., Maniezzo, V., Colorni, A.: Ant system: optimization by a colony of cooperating agents. IEEE Transactions on Systems, Man, and Cybernetics, Part b (cybernetics) **26**(1), 29–41 (1996)
3. Karaboga, D.: An Idea Based on Honey Bee Swarm for Numerical Optimization (2005)
4. Mirjalili, S., Lewis, A.: The whale optimization algorithm. Adv. Eng. Softw. **95**, 51–67 (2016)
5. Yang, X.S.: Firefly algorithms for multimodal optimization. In: International Symposium on Stochastic Algorithms, pp. 169–178 (2009). Springer Berlin Heidelberg, Berlin, Heidelberg
6. Aghakhani, S., Larijani, A., Sadeghi, F., Martín, D., Shahrakht, A.A.: A Novel hybrid artificial bee colony-based deep convolutional neural network to improve the detection performance of backscatter communication systems. Electronics **12**(10), 2263 (2023)
7. Karaman, A., et al.: Robust real-time polyp detection system design based on YOLO algorithms by optimizing activation functions and hyper-parameters with artificial bee colony (ABC). Expert Syst. Appl. **221**, 119741 (2023)
8. Ghaffar, M.A., Peng, L., Aslam, M.U., Adeel, M., Dassari, S.: Vehicle-UAV integrated routing optimization problem for emergency delivery of medical supplies. Electronics **13**(18), 3650 (2024)
9. Abro, A.G., Mohamad-Saleh, J.: Intelligent scout-bee based artificial bee colony optimization algorithm. In: 2012 IEEE International Conference on Control System, Computing and Engineering, pp. 380–385 (2012). IEEE
10. Gao, W., Liu, S., Huang, L.: A global best artificial bee colony algorithm for global optimization. J. Comput. Appl. Math. **236**(11), 2741–2753 (2012)
11. Pan, X., Lu, Y., Li, S., Li, R.: An improved artificial bee colony with new search strategy. Int. J. Wireless Mobile Comput. **9**(4), 391–396 (2015)
12. Wang, H., Wang, W., Xiao, S., Cui, Z., Xu, M., Zhou, X.: Improving artificial bee colony algorithm using a new neighborhood selection mechanism. Inf. Sci. **527**, 227–240 (2020)
13. Wang, Y., Jiao, J., Liu, J., Xiao, R.: A labor division artificial bee colony algorithm based on behavioral development. Inf. Sci. **606**, 152–172 (2022)
14. Ye, T., et al.: An improved two-archive artificial bee colony algorithm for many-objective optimization. Expert Syst. Appl. **236**, 121281 (2024)
15. Zhao, M., Wang, M.: Artificial bee colony algorithm with dynamic dimension search. In: 2024 3rd International Conference on Cloud Computing, Big Data Application and Software Engineering (CBASE), pp. 54–60 (2024). IEEE

16. Song, X., Zhang, X., Zhao, M.: Improved artificial bee colony algorithm embedded with differential evolution operator. In: 2024 9th International Conference on Electronic Technology and Information Science (ICETIS), pp. 716–719 (2024). IEEE
17. Cao, Y., Wang, X., Han, Z.: Multi-population artificial bee colony algorithm based on Lagrange interpolation. In: 2024 4th International Conference on Communication Technology and Information Technology (ICCTIT), pp. 665–670 (2024). IEEE
18. Li, S., Zhang, W., Hao, J., Li, R., Chen, J.: Artificial bee colony algorithm based on improved search strategy. In: International Conference on AI and Mobile Services, pp. 3–14 (2023). Springer Nature Switzerland, Cham
19. Yao, X., Liu, Y., Lin, G.: Evolutionary programming made faster. IEEE Trans. Evol. Comput. **3**(2), 82–102 (1999)

# Hybrid BERT-BiLSTM Model for SQL Injection Detection: Potential Applications in Banking Information Systems

Truong Cong Doan[1(✉)], Phan Thanh Duc[2], and Tran Van Loi[2]

[1] International School, Vietnam National University, Hanoi, Vietnam
tcdoan@vnu.edu.vn

[2] Faculty of Information Technology and Digital Economics, Banking Academy of Vietnam, Hanoi, Vietnam
{ducpt,loitv}@hvnh.edu.vn

**Abstract.** In banking information systems, databases containing customer information, contracts, and transactions play a critical role. However, these databases are increasingly targeted by cyberattacks aimed at stealing sensitive information. Among these threats, SQL injection (SQLi) remains one of the most prevalent cybersecurity risks to web applications and databases in banking systems, necessitating the development of advanced detection strategies to mitigate potential damage. To address this issue, artificial intelligence (AI) has emerged as a powerful tool for detecting SQLi attacks. This study proposes a novel hybrid model that integrates BERT (Bidirectional Encoder Representations from Transformers) and BiLSTM (Bidirectional Long Short-Term Memory) networks, leveraging BERT's contextual understanding and LSTM's ability to capture sequential dependencies for highly effective and accurate SQLi detection. The research utilizes a publicly available and widely adopted benchmark dataset containing 30,609 labeled SQL queries, including 19,268 benign queries and 11,341 SQLi queries. Several essential preprocessing steps, such as tokenization, noise removal, and normalization, were applied before model training to enhance data quality. Experimental results demonstrate that the proposed BERT-BiLSTM hybrid model outperforms existing techniques, including Decision Trees, Support Vector Machines (SVM), RNN, CNN-BiLSTM, and DNN-RHM, achieving an accuracy of 0.9994, precision of 0.9995, recall of 0.9991, and an F1-score of 0.9993. These findings highlight the model's potential for real-world deployment, strengthening system defense mechanisms, reducing the risk of data breaches, and improving compliance with cybersecurity standards. By integrating advanced contextual and sequential learning techniques, the proposed model provides a scalable and adaptable solution for enhancing the security of web applications and databases in banking information systems.

**Keywords:** SQL injection · banking information systems · Database · web application security · BERT · BiLSTM · Machine learning · Deep learning

# 1 Introduction

Artificial intelligence (AI) has advanced rapidly in recent years, finding applications across various domains such as banking, finance, education, and healthcare. Its integration aims to drive significant breakthroughs in these systems, enhancing efficiency, accuracy, and security. Banking information systems are no exception, as AI is increasingly applied to key challenges, including customer credit scoring, loan recommendations, fraud detection, and other financial services. Among these challenges, defending against SQL Injection (SQLi) attacks remains a critical concern in banking information systems. The rapid expansion of web applications and big data in recent years has led to a surge in cybersecurity threats, with SQLi attacks being one of the most persistent and severe vulnerabilities. According to the OWASP Top 10 report, SQL Injection continues to be the most prevalent type of web-based attack. These attacks exploit input fields by injecting malicious SQL code, allowing attackers to illegally access, modify, or delete data from underlying databases. A global security survey analyzing 300,000 web-based attacks found that approximately 24.6% were SQL Injection attacks, highlighting the urgency of developing effective detection and prevention mechanisms [1].

Traditional detection techniques, particularly rule-based systems, have proven limited in scope as they typically rely on predefined patterns and struggle to detect newly crafted malicious SQL queries [1]. These approaches often fail to adapt to the dynamic and evolving nature of modern SQLi techniques. As attackers continuously develop novel obfuscation and bypass strategies, the limitations of conventional methods become increasingly evident. To address these shortcomings, machine learning (ML) approaches have been explored for their ability to detect anomalies in SQL queries beyond hard-coded patterns. Classical ML models [2, 3] such as Decision Trees, Support Vector Machines (SVM), Logistic Regression, Naive Bayes, and K-Nearest Neighbor have been utilized to classify SQL queries based on engineered features. J. Triloka [4], for instance, conducted a comparative study of five classical algorithms Naive Bayes, Logistic Regression, Gradient Boosting, SVM, and KNN and found that SVM produced the highest classification accuracy among them. However, despite their relative success, these models often fall short in capturing the contextual semantics of SQL statements and lack the robustness required for detecting complex, adversarial query patterns.

Several other studies [5–9] have applied machine learning techniques and reported reasonable performance across standard evaluation metrics such as accuracy, precision, recall, and F1-score. Nevertheless, many of these models struggle with generalizability and robustness, particularly when faced with previously unseen or obfuscated SQLi queries. These limitations underscore the need for more adaptive and context-aware detection models. Beyond classical ML, researchers have explored various strategies to improve detection effectiveness. For example, Moissinac et al. [10] proposed a feature engineering approach that integrates SQL and HTTP language mixtures to improve SQLi detection while reducing annotation workload. However, this technique still suffers from false positives, limiting its real-world practicality. Another method involving real-time SQLi detection through server log monitoring [11] introduces additional operational overhead due to the constant logging requirement, posing challenges in data synchronization and system performance.

In the realm of deep learning, Alghawazi et al. [8] proposed a deep learning architecture using an RNN autoencoder to detect SQL injection attacks. Their model achieved 94% accuracy and 92% F1-score. Their model outperformed several traditional machine learning classifiers. Similarly, N. Gandhi et al. [1] proposed a hybrid CNN-BiLSTM model that achieved 98% accuracy by combining CNN's feature extraction capabilities with BiLSTM's contextual understanding. While this method outperformed traditional approaches, this model still struggled with highly dynamic SQLi patterns in real-world scenarios. Jothi. K. R et al. [12] proposed a Multilayer Perceptron (MLP) model incorporating an embedding layer and multiple dense layers to detect SQL injection attacks, achieving an accuracy of 98%. A closely related work by Y. Liu and Y. Dai [9] presented a hybrid BERT–LSTM model that leverages BERT's contextual embedding capabilities alongside a unidirectional LSTM for temporal modeling. Their model incorporated dimensionality reduction (768 → 128), dropout (0.5), and feature fusion via concatenation of the [CLS] token with LSTM outputs. The preprocessing pipeline included tokenization, padding, attention masking, and encoding techniques to handle obfuscated queries, achieving 97.3% accuracy, 96.3% precision, 96.2% recall, and 95.8% F1-score. In a different line of research, Nguyen et al. [13] introduced a novel graph convolutional network named Refined Highway Module (RHM), which achieved the highest reported accuracy of 99.91%. Despite its high performance, the approach requires quite complex model design and additional computational costs.

In light of these developments, this study proposes an improved hybrid architecture that combines BERT with Bidirectional Long Short-Term Memory (BiLSTM) networks to detect SQL injection attacks with higher accuracy and efficiency. Unlike previous approaches that rely on complex dimensionality reduction or feature fusion techniques, our method maintains a simplified structure while leveraging BERT's bidirectional contextual understanding and BiLSTM's sequential modeling capabilities. We utilize a benchmark dataset comprising 30,609 labeled SQL queries including 19,268 benign and 11,341 malicious which used in academic research and competitions widely. A lightweight preprocessing pipeline, including tokenization, noise removal, and normalization, is applied to enhance the quality of input data. Our optimized BERT-BiLSTM model achieves outstanding results: 0.9994 accuracy, 0.9995 precision, 0.9991 recall, and 0.9993 F1-score, outperforming traditional and state-of-the-art methods such as Decision Tree, SVM, RNN, CNN-BiLSTM, and BERT-LSTM. In summary, we propose a lightweight yet highly accurate hybrid BERT-BiLSTM architecture for SQLi detection. We demonstrate that high performance can be achieved without dimensionality reduction or complex feature engineering. We provide a comprehensive evaluation against traditional and deep learning baselines on a widely adopted SQLi dataset. This proposal is very important in preventing hacker attacks especially in banking information systems.

## 2 Methodology

### 2.1 Dataset and Preprocessing

#### 2.1.1 Dataset Description

The dataset used in this study comprises 30,609 labeled SQL queries sourced from Kaggle competitions focused on SQL injection classification. It has been downloaded over 10,000 times and is widely adopted by the data science community for benchmarking SQLi detection models. Each entry includes a `Query` representing an SQL statement and a corresponding `Label` indicating whether it is benign or a SQL injection.

#### 2.1.2 Label Cleaning

Input data was cleaned to ensure that all labels were converted to standardized integer types. SQL queries with missing or malformed labels were removed to facilitate proper model training. After label normalization, stopwords that did not affect the semantics or syntax of SQL statements were filtered out. The dataset contains two primary columns: `Query` (the SQL statement) and `Label` (indicating whether it is an SQL injection or not).

#### 2.1.3 Tokenization and Stopword Removal

Unlike conventional stopword removal in NLP, filtering stopwords in SQL queries requires caution to preserve semantically important tokens. To prevent the loss of contextual information essential for classification, we adopted the following approach. First, we utilized an uppercase English stopword list from the Natural Language Toolkit (NLTK) as a base. This list was then manually refined to retain critical SQL keywords, including 'SELECT', 'FROM', 'WHERE', 'AND', 'OR', 'NOT', 'UNION', 'JOIN', 'INSERT', 'UPDATE', 'DELETE', 'DROP', 'CREATE', 'ALTER', 'TABLE', 'INTO', 'VALUES', 'SET', 'GROUP', 'BY', 'ORDER', 'HAVING', 'DISTINCT', 'LIMIT', 'OFFSET', 'LIKE', 'IN', 'EXISTS', 'BETWEEN', 'NULL', 'IS', 'CASE', 'WHEN', 'THEN', 'ELSE', 'END', 'AS' To ensure consistency and eliminate case sensitivity, all SQL queries were converted to uppercase. Queries were then tokenized into word lists, and customized stopword removal was applied based on the refined list. Additionally, non-essential characters were removed while preserving valid SQL elements such as letters, digits, quotes, comparison operators, logical operators, and key symbols like;, /, *, and -. The resulting cleaned tokens were then concatenated to form normalized SQL queries, which were used as model input.

#### 2.1.4 SQL Dataset Encoding for BERT

We utilize the BERT-base-uncased model to extract contextual embeddings from SQL queries. Each query is encoded using the BertTokenizer through a series of steps: converting queries into token IDs, applying padding to ensure a fixed sequence length, generating attention masks to guide the model's focus, and returning 'input_ids' and 'attention_mask' tensors as inputs to the BERT model. This process is encapsulated within a custom dataset class, enabling seamless integration with the training pipeline.

### 2.1.5 Train/Validation/Test Split

After preprocessing, the dataset was divided into three subsets: 80% for training, 10% for validation (used for model tuning), and 10% for testing (used to evaluate generalisations based on unseen data). We applied a fixed random seed (random_state = 42) to ensure reproducibility.

## 2.2 Proposed Model Architecture

The proposed model is a hybrid architecture combining Bidirectional Encoder Representations from Transformers (BERT) with a Bidirectional Long Short-Term Memory network (BiLSTM). This design builds upon the work of Liu et al. [9], with enhancements that improve both accuracy and generalizability (Fig. 1).

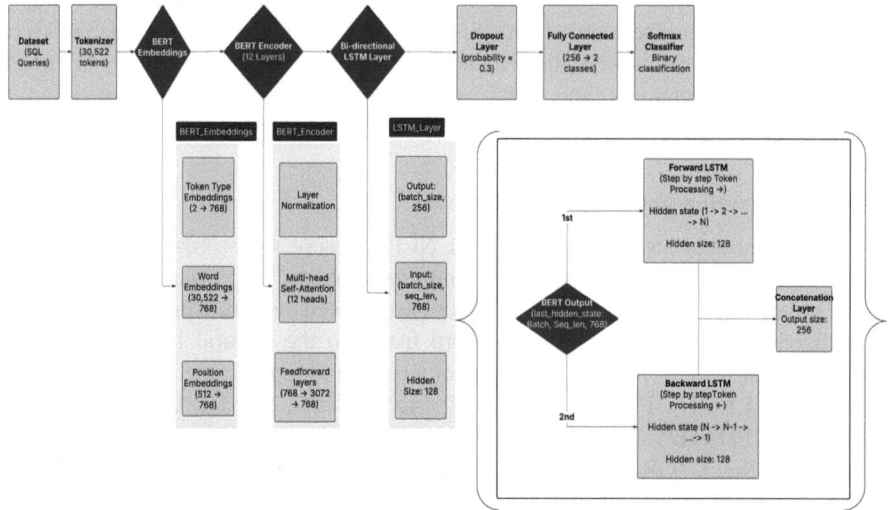

**Fig. 1.** BERT-BiLSTM proposed model architecture

### 2.2.1 BERT Embedding Layer

We utilize the pre-trained BERT-base-uncased model to extract contextual embeddings for each SQL query. Queries are first tokenized using the BertTokenizer, then converted into token IDs with padding and attention masks applied. These tensors (input_ids and attention_mask) are used as input to BERT, which outputs hidden representations of each token in the sequence.

### 2.2.2 BiLSTM Layer

The output embeddings from BERT are passed into a bidirectional LSTM layer. Unlike unidirectional LSTM, BiLSTM processes sequences in both forward and backward directions, capturing richer contextual information. This helps the model detect subtle and obfuscated SQLi patterns.

### 2.2.3 Fully Connected Layer and Softmax

The final hidden states from the BiLSTM are concatenated and passed through a fully connected dense layer followed by a softmax activation function to classify SQL queries into two categories: benign or malicious.

### 2.2.4 Proposed Improvements

- The Preprocessing Enhancement: We apply SQL-specific stopword filtering that removes irrelevant tokens while retaining crucial SQL keywords such as SELECT, FROM, WHERE, etc.
- Hyperparameter Optimization: In contrast to Liu et al. [9], who used a fixed learning rate of 0.01, we adopt an adaptive strategy using a learning rate of 2e-5 combined with a StepLR scheduler that reduces the rate by 10% every 3 epochs. Other hyperparameters include a batch size of 16 and a dropout rate of 0.3.

These improvements contribute to higher accuracy and better generalization on unseen, real-world SQLi examples.

## 3 Performance Evaluation

### 3.1 Evaluation Metrics

To evaluate the model's performance, we utilize four standard classification metrics: Accuracy, Precision, Recall, and F1-score. Accuracy measures the proportion of correct predictions, while Precision represents the ratio of true positives (TP) to total predicted positives (TP + FP), indicating the reliability of positive predictions. Recall is the ratio of TP to actual positives (TP + FN), assessing the model's ability to detect all relevant instances. The F1-score, defined as the harmonic mean of Precision and Recall, provides a balanced measure between the two. These metrics (Table 1) are mathematically defined as follows:

**Table 1.** Evalation Metrics

| Metrics | Formula |
|---|---|
| Precision (P): | $P = \frac{TP}{TP+FP}$ |
| Recall (R) | $R = \frac{TP}{TP+FN}$ |
| Accuracy (Acc) | $Acc = \frac{TP+TN}{TP+FN+TN+FP}$ |
| F1-score (F1) | $F1 = 2\frac{P*R}{P+R} = \frac{2TP}{2TP+FN+FP}$ |

These metrics collectively provide a comprehensive evaluation of the model's ability to accurately detect SQL injection attacks while minimizing false alarms.

## 4 Results

### 4.1 Experimental Setup

The experiment was conducted using a benchmark dataset of 30,609 SQL queries, each labeled as either benign or a SQL injection. Data preprocessing involved removing unwanted characters, converting all text to uppercase, and filtering out non-essential stopwords while preserving critical SQL keywords. The dataset was then split into 80% training, 10% validation, and 10% testing, using a fixed random seed (random_state = 42) to ensure reproducibility.

For encoding, we employed the bert-base-uncased tokenizer from Hugging Face Transformers to convert each query into input_ids and attention_mask tensors. These tokenized inputs were processed using a PyTorch-compatible data pipeline for efficient loading and training, with sequences padded or truncated to a maximum length of 128 tokens. The proposed model integrates BERT for contextual embeddings with a bidirectional LSTM (BiLSTM) to capture both forward and backward dependencies within the query structure. The output is passed through a dropout layer (dropout rate: 0.3), followed by a fully connected layer with softmax activation for binary classification. The model was trained on a GPU with the following settings:

- Batch size: 16
- Learning rate: 2e-5, adjusted using a StepLR scheduler (reducing the rate by 10% every 3 epochs)
- Optimizer: Adam
- Loss function: CrossEntropyLoss
- Epochs: 5

Throughout training and evaluation, we monitored performance using standard metrics: accuracy, precision, recall, and F1-score. Final evaluation on the test set confirmed the model's effectiveness in detecting both standard and obfuscated SQL injection queries.

### 4.2 Comparison with Baseline Methods

Table 2. Performance Comparison of Deep Learning Approaches

| Model | Accuracy | Precision | Recall | F1 |
|---|---|---|---|---|
| RNN-Autoencoder [6] | 0.9400 | - | - | 0.9200 |
| CNN-BiLSTM [1] | 0.9800 | - | - | - |
| Multilayer Perceptron (MLP) [12] | 0.9800 | 0.9800 | 0.9700 | 0.9750 |
| BERT-LSTM [9] | 0.9730 | 0.9630 | 0.9620 | 0.9580 |
| DNN-RHM [13] | 0.9993 | 0.9991 | 0.9991 | 0.9991 |
| **Our proposed Model** | **0.9994** | **0.9995** | **0.9991** | **0.9993** |

While various classical machine learning models (e.g., SVM, Decision Trees, etc.) were included in preliminary experiments, deep learning approaches significantly outperformed them. Therefore, we focus our comparison on recent deep learning architectures, as shown in Table 2. As a result, our BERT-BiLSTM architecture achieves the highest overall performance across all evaluation metrics.

## 5 Conclusion

In this study, we proposed a hybrid deep learning model that combines BERT and Bidirectional LSTM (BiLSTM) to detect SQL injection (SQLi) attacks with high accuracy and robustness. By leveraging BERT's contextual understanding and BiLSTM's sequential learning capabilities, the model effectively identifies malicious SQL queries, including those with obfuscation or complex structures. Through extensive preprocessing, tokenization, and model optimization, our approach achieved state-of-the-art performance with an accuracy of 0.9994, precision of 0.9995, recall of 0.9991, and F1-score of 0.9993. These results surpass the performance of traditional machine learning models and several recent deep learning architectures. The findings demonstrate that the BERT-BiLSTM model not only improves detection accuracy but also reduces false positives, making it suitable for real-world applications in web security systems. Future work may explore integrating attention-based mechanisms, deploying the model in production environments, or extending the approach to detect other types of injection attacks.

## References

1. Gandhi, N., Patel, J., Sisodiya, R., Doshi, N., Mishra, S.: A CNN-BiLSTM based approach for detection of SQL injection attacks. In: International Conference on Computational Intelligence and Knowledge Economy (ICCIKE), pp. 378–383 (2021). https://doi.org/10.1109/ICCIKE51210.2021.9410675
2. Doan, T.C., Linh, B.K., Linh, T.K., Trang, N.Q., Oanh, N.T.K.: AI-driven URL classification for targeted advertising in the digital era. In: Gartner, W. (ed.) New Perspectives and Paradigms in Applied Economics and Business, pp. 181–194 (2025). Springer Nature Switzerland, Cham. https://doi.org/10.1007/978-3-031-77363-1_13
3. Truong, C.D., Nguyen, V.C., Kim Oanh, N.T.: Estimating smartphone price ranges using machine learning models. In: Nguyen, T.D.L., Dawson, M., Ngoc, L.A., Lam, K.Y. (eds.) Proceedings of the International Conference on Intelligent Systems and Networks, pp. 697–707 (2024). Springer Nature, Singapore. https://doi.org/10.1007/978-981-97-5504-2_80
4. Triloka, J., Hartono, H., Sutedi, S.: Detection of SQL injection attack using machine learning based on natural language processing. International Journal of Artificial Intelligence Research 6 (2022). https://doi.org/10.29099/ijair.v6i2.355
5. Hosam, E., Hosny, H., Ashraf, W., Kaseb, A.S.: SQL injection detection using machine learning techniques. In: 8th International Conference on Soft Computing & Machine Intelligence (ISCMI), pp. 15–20 (2021). https://doi.org/10.1109/ISCMI53840.2021.9654820
6. Alghawazi, M., Alghazzawi, D., Alarifi, S.: Detection of SQL injection attack using machine learning techniques: a systematic literature review. Journal of Cybersecurity and Privacy 2, 764–777 (2022). https://doi.org/10.3390/jcp2040039

7. Gupta, A., Tyagi, L.K., Mohamed, A.: A machine learning methodology for detecting SQL injection attacks. In: 3rd International Conference on Technological Advancements in Computational Sciences (ICTACS) (2023). https://doi.org/10.1109/ICTACS59847.2023.10390153
8. Alghawazi, M., Alghazzawi, D., Alarifi, S.: Deep learning architecture for detecting SQL injection attacks based on RNN Autoencoder model. Mathematics **11**, 3286 (2023). https://doi.org/10.3390/math11153286
9. Liu, Y., Dai, Y.: Deep Learning in Cybersecurity: A Hybrid BERT–LSTM Network for SQL Injection Attack Detection. Article ID 5565950 (2024). https://doi.org/10.1049/2024/5565950
10. Moissinac, B., Saad, E., Clay, M., Berrondo, M.: Detecting SQL injection attacks using machine learning. In: CAMLIS'23: Conference on Applied Machine Learning for Information Security (2023)
11. Azman, M.A.: Others: machine learning-based technique to detect SQL injection attack. J. Comput. Sci. **17**, 296–303 (2021). https://doi.org/10.3844/jcssp.2021.296.303
12. Balaj, J.K., Pandey, N., Beriwal, P., Amarajan, A.: An efficient SQL injection detection system using deep learning. In: ICCIKE, pp. 442–445 (2021). https://doi.org/10.1109/ICCIKE51210.2021.9410674
13. Nguyen, D.C., Ha, M.H., Chen, O.T.C., Do, M.T.: RHM: novel graph convolution based on non-local network for SQL injection identification. In: IEEE Symposium on Industrial Electronics & Applications (ISIEA), pp. 1–5 (2024). https://doi.org/10.1109/ISIEA61920.2024.10607303

# AC-Net: An Adaptive Step-Size Low-Light Image Enhancement Method Based on Global Illumination Modeling

Xiuqin Pan[✉], Yiqun Wang, and Xuze Gu

Minzu University of China, Haidian District, 27 Zhongguancun South Street, Beijing, China
amycun@163.com

**Abstract.** Low-light image enhancement is vital for computer vision, yet existing methods like Zero-DCE have drawbacks: their fixed-step recursive enhancement often causes over-or insufficient enhancement, and ReLU's non-smoothness leads to abrupt brightness transitions and gradient vanishing in extremely dark regions, limiting fine-detail recovery. To solve these issues, this paper proposes the AC-Net low-light enhancement network with two key innovations. First, a feature extraction module based on smooth nonlinear mapping replaces ReLU with Softplus—this improves illumination transition smoothness and mitigates gradient vanishing. Combined with a U-Net encoder–decoder structure and skip connections, it enables multi-scale feature fusion and high-quality image reconstruction. Second, an adaptive enhancement step-size module extracts a global illumination descriptor vector from shared features; a fully connected layer predicts enhancement strength ratios, and a probabilistic sampling mechanism maps these ratios to discrete steps (larger steps for darker areas to ensure sufficient detail enhancement, smaller steps for brighter regions to avoid overexposure). AC-Net produces enhanced images with smoother illumination, fewer artifacts/color distortions, and richer high-frequency details. Experiments on public datasets show it outperforms state-of-the-art methods in PSNR, SSIM, and LPIPS, with stability in cross-domain scenarios (e.g., UIEB underwater dataset). Ablation experiments further verify each module's role in performance improvement.

**Keywords:** low-light image enhancement · smooth nonlinear mapping activation function · adaptive step size · global illumination modeling

## 1 Introduction

With the rapid development of computer vision, high-quality images have become of great importance in areas such as surveillance, object detection, face recognition, satellite remote sensing, and medical imaging. However, images captured under nighttime, backlight, adverse weather, or other uncontrollable low-light conditions often suffer from insufficient or uneven illumination, low contrast, color degradation, and noise interference. Such degraded images significantly undermine the robustness and performance of tasks like object detection and image recognition, thereby making low-light image enhancement (LLIE) an active research topic in computer vision. At present, LLIE methods can be broadly categorized into two groups: traditional methods and deep learning–based methods.

## 1.1 Traditional Methods

Traditional methods mainly include model-based approaches and data-driven approaches, the latter of which can be roughly divided into Retinex-based methods and histogram equalization (HE)–based methods. Retinex theory, proposed by Land [1] in 1963, models the human visual system's perception of uneven illumination. Retinex methods enhance image brightness and contrast by estimating and correcting the illumination component so that the reflection component more closely resembles the true object properties in the scene. HE, on the other hand, enhances image contrast by remapping pixel values using the cumulative distribution function of the input image to achieve a more uniform distribution. Guo et al. [2] introduced a simple yet effective LLIE approach by estimating the maximum channel value of each pixel to construct an initial illumination map, followed by optimization with structural priors to improve visibility. However, these traditional methods generally struggle to adapt to complex illumination conditions, often resulting in color distortion, over-enhancement, or loss of details, and they lack adaptability across different scenes.

## 1.2 Deep Learning-Based Methods

Deep learning–based LLIE methods can be classified into supervised learning, unsupervised learning, and zero-shot learning.

### Supervised Learning Methods
In 2017, Lore et al. [3] proposed LLNet, the first work to introduce deep neural networks into LLIE. LLNet employed stacked auto encoders (SAE) to learn hierarchical features from low-light images, thereby simultaneously improving brightness and reducing noise. Inspired by Retinex theory, Yang et al. [4] developed an end-to-end framework that combines prior-guided layer decomposition with data-driven mapping for single-image low-light enhancement.

### Unsupervised and Zero-Shot Learning Methods
The aforementioned supervised learning–based LLIE methods require paired low- and normal-light images for training. To alleviate the dependency of deep models on paired datasets, increasing research attention has been given to unsupervised and zero-shot learning approaches in recent years.

Guo et al. proposed Zero-DCE [5], a reference-free deep curve estimation method that formulates illumination enhancement as an image-adaptive curve estimation task. By training a lightweight network (DCE-Net), Zero-DCE estimates high-order curves at the pixel level to adjust the dynamic range of the image. This method eliminates the need for paired or unpaired training data by leveraging carefully designed reference-free loss functions. To further improve inference efficiency while maintaining performance, the authors later introduced an accelerated version, Zero-DCE++ [6], which reduces computational complexity. These approaches avoid manual data annotation and reduce training costs; however, the absence of explicit learning objectives often leads to issues such as detail loss [7] and color degradation [8].

In summary, LLIE research has evolved from traditional approaches such as histogram equalization and Retinex-based methods to deep learning–based end-to-end solutions, including KinD, LEES-Net, and Zero-DCE. In particular, Zero-DCE significantly reduces annotation costs while maintaining high-quality enhancement by proposing a reference-free curve estimation strategy that does not rely on paired training data. Nevertheless, Zero-DCE still suffers from two major limitations:

(1) Zero-DCE employs ReLU as the activation function, which may cause gradient vanishing in extremely dark regions and thereby limit enhancement effectiveness. Moreover, the non-smooth nature of ReLU can produce abrupt transitions in brightness, reducing the naturalness of the enhanced image.
(2) Zero-DCE relies on a fixed recursive step size, whereas the optimal number of enhancement iterations should vary dynamically across different low-light images. A fixed step size can thus lead to under-enhancement or over-enhancement, degrading overall image quality.

To overcome these limitations, this paper proposes a novel adaptive step-size–based low-light image enhancement framework, termed Adaptive Curve Network (AC-Net). The main contributions are as follows:

(1) A feature extraction module based on smooth nonlinear mapping is designed, where Softplus replaces ReLU as the activation function to mitigate gradient vanishing in extremely dark regions and improve curve smoothness, enabling more natural brightness transitions in the enhanced images.
(2) An adaptive enhancement step-size module is introduced, which predicts the number of enhancement iterations adaptively via global feature–based estimation. This enables dynamic adjustment of the enhancement process according to the input image, ensuring more accurate brightness correction while reducing computational overhead.
(3) Extensive experiments conducted on the LOLv2 dataset demonstrate that AC-Net significantly outperforms multiple state-of-the-art LLIE methods in terms of PSNR, SSIM, and LPIPS, thereby validating the superior performance of the proposed approach.

## 2 Adaptive Step-Size Method Based on Global Illumination Modeling

To address the limitations of Zero-DCE in low-light image enhancement—namely, the non-smooth activation function that degrades the naturalness of brightness transitions and the fixed enhancement step size that reduces flexibility—this paper proposes an improved Zero-DCE architecture, termed AC-Net. The model mainly consists of two modules: (1) a feature extraction module based on smooth nonlinear activation mapping, which enhances the naturalness of brightness transitions; and (2) an adaptive enhancement step-size module, which improves the flexibility of iterative enhancement.

## 2.1 Feature Extraction Module Based on Smooth Nonlinear Activation Mapping

In the original Zero-DCE architecture [9], ReLU was adopted as the activation function in DCE-Net to ensure the non-negativity of curve adjustment parameters. However, this design suffers from two critical issues in the context of low-light image enhancement:

(1) The non-smooth property of ReLU may lead to abrupt brightness transitions in the enhanced images, thereby degrading visual naturalness.
(2) When the input values are very small, ReLU can cause gradient vanishing, which limits the model's enhancement capability in extremely dark regions.

To address these drawbacks, this paper replaces ReLU with Softplus as the activation function. Softplus improves the smoothness of brightness transitions in the enhanced images and alleviates gradient vanishing, thereby enhancing the model's ability to recover details in very dark areas. The Softplus function is defined as:

$$f(x) = ln(1 + e^x) \qquad (1)$$

$A_t$ derivative is given in Eq. (2),

$$f'(x) = \frac{1}{1 + e^x} \qquad (2)$$

As can be observed, Softplus maintains a small positive gradient even when x < 0, which effectively alleviates the gradient vanishing problem of ReLU in the negative domain. Moreover, Softplus exhibits superior smoothness, enabling the predicted curve parameters to remain more stable and reducing abrupt brightness transitions during the enhancement process.

In the Zero-DCE framework, DCE-Net is responsible for predicting the pixel-wise adjustment curve parameters $A_t$, which are computed as:

$$J = I + \sum_{t+1}^{T} A_t \cdot I \cdot (1 - I) \qquad (3)$$

Here, A is computed by DCE-Net as shown in Eq. (4),

$$A_t = \text{Softplus}(W_t * I + b_t) \qquad (4)$$

where $W_t$ and $b_t$ denote the convolutional weights and biases of DCE-Net, respectively, and * represents the convolution operation. Since Softplus consistently outputs positive values, it ensures more stable predictions of A by DCE-Net, thereby enhancing the overall enhancement performance while reducing image noise and artifacts, resulting in more natural outputs.

Therefore, this paper replaces ReLU with Softplus as the activation function and proposes a feature extraction module based on smooth nonlinear activation mapping for low-light image enhancement tasks. In terms of the overall architecture, the network inherits the typical U-Net symmetric encoder-decoder structure and incorporates skip connections to achieve multi-scale feature fusion. The use of Softplus in place of the conventional ReLU effectively alleviates the problem of gradient sparsity and enhances nonlinear representation capability. At the end of the decoding stage, a shallow feature reconstruction module is introduced, which leverages multiple convolutional layers to strengthen the extraction and recovery of local detail information. Meanwhile, during decoding, $2 \times 2$ transposed convolutions (Up-conv) are adopted to replace traditional up sampling operations, enabling the recovery of image resolution while better preserving structural information.

These improvements significantly enhance the network's capability for feature reconstruction and image restoration under complex environments, thus laying a solid foundation for subsequent high-quality image enhancement. The structure of the proposed feature extraction module based on smooth nonlinear activation mapping is illustrated in Fig. 1.

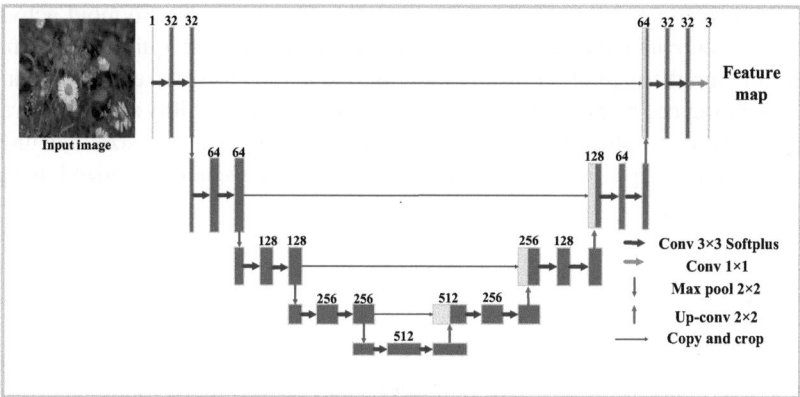

**Fig. 1.** Feature extraction module based on smooth nonlinear mapping activation function

### 2.2 Adaptive Enhancement Step Size

In the traditional Zero-DCE module, the input low-light image is enhanced pixel by pixel through curve adjustment, and the transition from a low-light state to an ideal brightness is gradually achieved through iterative processing. Image enhancement is realized by recursively applying the adjustment curve $T$ times, where $T$ is a fixed value, as shown in Eq. (5):

$$I_{t+1}^{(h)} = I_t^{(h)} + A_t^{(h)} \cdot I_t^{(h)} \cdot (1 - I_t^{(h)}), t = 0, 1, \ldots, T - 1 \tag{5}$$

Here, $I_0^{(h)} = I$ denotes the initial input low-light image, and $A_t^{(h)}$ represents the adjustment parameters predicted by the $h$-th enhancement head at the $t$-th iteration. However, there exist significant differences in illumination distribution and detail degradation among different low-light images: for images with fewer details and extremely low brightness, more iterative steps may be required to achieve satisfactory enhancement; whereas for images with richer details orpartially brighter regions, a fixed step size $T$ may lead to over-enhancement or unnecessary computational overhead.

To address this issue, this paper introduces an Adaptive Enhancement Step Module (AESM). AESM enables the model to dynamically estimate an appropriate step size

$T$ according to the global illumination characteristics of the low-light image, thereby achieving better control of the enhancement process so that the final output image is neither lacking in details nor overexposed. First, the shared features $T$ extracted by DCE-Net are used to obtain global illumination information, i.e., by applying global average pooling to obtain a global descriptive vector, as shown in Eq. (6):

$$f_{GAP} = \frac{1}{H \times W} \sum_{i=1}^{H} \sum_{j=1}^{W} F(i,j) \in R^C \quad (6)$$

Subsequently, a fully connected layer is used to map the global features into a scalar $s$:

$$s = \sigma(W_T \cdot f_{GAP} + b_T) \quad (7)$$

where $W_T$ and $b_t$ are learnable parameters, and $\sigma(\cdot)$ denotes the Sigmoid activation function. The output s indicates the overall enhancement intensity required for the image. In order to map the prediction results into discrete iterative step sizes while reducing the errors introduced by discretization, this paper adopts a probability sampling strategy based on continuous prediction values. The maximum iterative step size is defined as $T_{max}$ ($T_{max}$ is an integer), and the actual enhancement step size is quantized using the following formula:

$$T = T_{max} \quad (8)$$

Definition:

$$k = \lfloor T \rfloor, p = T - k \quad (9)$$

Equation (9) decomposes $T$ into an integer part $k$ and a fractional part $p$, where with probability $p$, the enhancement is performed $k + 1$ times, and with probability $1 - p$, the enhancement is performed $k$ times, i.e.:

$$T = \begin{cases} k + 1, & \text{with probability } p \\ k, & \text{with probalility } 1 - p \end{cases} \quad (10)$$

The probability sampling strategy based on continuous prediction values can effectively alleviate the abrupt step size changes caused by discretization, improve the stability and refinement of the enhancement strategy, and ensure that the actual enhancement step size $T$ is an integer. The adaptive enhancement step size strategy proposed in this paper enables:

(1) For regions with higher brightness or richer local details, the model predicts a smaller step size $T$ avoiding over-enhancement, saving computational resources, and preventing overexposure;
(2) For images with overall low brightness or fewer local details, the model adaptively predicts a larger step size $T$, thereby performing multiple iterative enhancements to achieve better enhancement results.

The AESM module can work synergistically with the feature extraction module based on the smooth nonlinear mapping activation function, ensuring the smoothness of the enhancement curve. As a result, the final output images exhibit more natural and stable performance in terms of color, brightness, and detail. The entire network is named the Multi-Head Adaptive Curve Network (AC-Net).

## 3 Experimental Results and Analysis

### 3.1 Experimental Dataset

(1) LOLv2 [12] is currently the authoritative benchmark dataset in the field of low-light image enhancement. It includes both real and synthetic subsets and contains various forms of image degradation such as extremely low brightness, uneven illumination, and noise. The real subset consists of 689 training images and 100 testing images, while the synthetic subset contains 900 training images and 100 testing images. This dataset is widely used for algorithm training and evaluation, providing a unified standard and generalization benchmark for performance comparison under complex low-light conditions.

(2) UIEB. To verify the generalization ability of the model, this paper conducted further experiments using the UIEB dataset. The UIEB dataset is currently one of the most widely used benchmark datasets in the field of underwater image enhancement. It was proposed by the Chinese Academy of Sciences Shenzhen Institute of Advanced Technology in 2019. The image is collected from the actual marine environment, covering various types of water bodies, lighting conditions, and underwater targets, and includes various typical underwater image problems such as color distortion, blur, low contrast, and high noise. A total of 890 manually annotated images were included. In this experiment, 790 images were randomly selected as the training set, and the remaining 100 images were used as the testing set.

### 3.2 Experimental Environment and Parameter Settings

Experiments were conducted under the Pytorch framework. The computing environment consisted of a Windows 11 operating system, an NVIDIA GeForce GTX 3060 GPU, a 12th Gen Intel(R) Core(TM) i7-12700H CPU, and 16.0 GB RAM. The Adaptive Enhancement Step Module adopts a global average pooling linear layer to predict the enhancement step size (normalized to [1, 10]). The model was trained using the Adam optimizer with an initial learning rate of 0.0001 for a total of 100 epochs.

### 3.3 Evaluation Metrics

PSNR, SSIM, and LPIPS were employed as evaluation metrics. Peak Signal-to-Noise Ratio (PSNR) mainly measures the pixel-level error between the enhanced image and the reference image, with its unit being decibels. The formula for PSNR is as follows:

$$PSNR = 10 \cdot log_{10}(\frac{MAX^2}{MSE}) \qquad (11)$$

SSIM (Structural Similarity Index) primarily measures similarity in terms of luminance, contrast, and structure, which aligns more closely with human visual perception. Its formula is as follows:

$$SSIM(x, y) = \frac{(2\mu_x\mu_y + C_1)(2\sigma_{xy} + C_2)}{(\mu_x^2 + \mu_y^2 + C_1)(\sigma_x^2 + \sigma_y^2 + C_2)} \qquad (12)$$

Learned Perceptual Image Patch Similarity (LPIPS) computes the difference between the enhanced image and the reference image in the high-level feature space using deep neural networks, which can better simulate the perceptual effects of the human visual system. It can be expressed as:

$$LPIPS(x, y) = \sum_{l} \omega_l \|\Phi_l(x) - \Phi_l(y)\|_2^2 \tag{13}$$

In summary, PSNR reflects pixel-level errors, SSIM measures structural similarity, and LPIPS evaluates perceptual quality. Together, these three metrics provide a comprehensive assessment of the effectiveness of a model in low-light image enhancement tasks.

### 3.4 Comparative Experiment

To verify the effectiveness of the AC-Net proposed in this article on publicly available low light datasets, a comparative experiment was conducted between the classic low light image enhancement model and the state-of-the-art method on the LOL dataset.

Initial image  KinD++  PairLIE  RetinexNet  EnlightenGAN  Zero-DCE  L²DM  Retinexformer  ours

**Fig. 2.** Comparison of Image Enhancement Effects between AC-Net and Classic Algorithms

From Fig. 2, it can be seen that in terms of visual effects, AC-Net performs outstandingly in dark area detail restoration, color balance, and noise suppression. Compared with Zero-DCE, RetinexFormer, L²DM and other methods, the enhanced images by AC-Net avoid overexposure and color distortion while maintaining image brightness improvement, presenting a more natural and realistic visual effect; Compared with classic methods such as RetinexNet and PairLIE, our method is more detailed in preserving edge structure and texture, significantly reducing blurring and artifacts, providing the most suitable brightness and contrast, the lowest distortion, and more high-frequency details and structures.

**Table 1.** Comparison of evaluation indicators between AC-Net and classical algorithms

| Model | PSNR↑ | SSIM↑ | LPIPS↓ |
|---|---|---|---|
| KinD++ [7] | 20.27 | 0.8397 | 0.1727 |
| PairLIE | 19.15 | 0.7401 | 0.3138 |
| RetinexNet | 19.46 | 0.8213 | 0.1566 |
| EnlightGAN [10] | 20.02 | 0.7824 | 0.1816 |
| Zero-DCE [9] | 22.68 | 0.8369 | 0.1258 |
| $L^2$DM [11] | 23.78 | 0.7858 | 0.1371 |
| Retinexformer [12] | 22.84 | 0.8385 | 0.1535 |
| AC-Net(ours) | **24.37** | **0.8619** | **0.1156** |

Quantitative results. Table 1 shows the performance comparison between AC-Net and various mainstream low light image enhancement methods on the LOLv2 dataset. It can be seen that AC-Net achieved the best performance in the three indicators of PSNR, SSIM, and LPIPS, with PSNR of 24.37 dB, which is improved compared to advanced models $L^2$DM (23.78 dB) and RetinexFormer (22.84 dB), indicating that the model has stronger robustness in restoring image details and suppressing noise. The SSIM index reached 0.8619, reflecting that the structure of AC-Net enhanced images is more complete and the texture is finer; The lowest LPIPS value(0.1156) indicates that AC-Net is closer to real images in terms of perceptual quality, and the enhancement results are more in line with human subjective perception. By integrating three evaluation indicators, the effectiveness and frontier of the AC-Net proposed in this paper in low light image enhancement tasks have been verified.

To verify the generalization ability of AC-Net, this paper further conducted cross domain testing on the UIEB dataset, which mainly includes underwater low light images with obvious cross modal and extreme lighting features. The experiment introduced multiple classic algorithms (such as RetinexNet, EnlightGAN [10], Zero DCE [9], etc.) and various state-of-the-art methods on the UIEB dataset (FDCE-Net [13], UIE-DM [14]), and conducted a comprehensive comparative analysis with the proposed method. The experimental results are shown in Table 2.

**Table 2.** Comparison of Evaluation Metrics between AC-Net and Classic Algorithms on UIEB Dataset

| Model | PSNR↑ | SSIM↑ | LPIPS↓ |
|---|---|---|---|
| KinD++ [7] | 18.49 | 0.8257 | 0.1707 |
| PairLIE | 18.51 | 0.7805 | 0.2865 |
| RetinexNet | 18.86 | 0.8343 | 0.1581 |
| EnlightGAN [10] | 22.26 | 0.8403 | 0.1025 |

(*continued*)

Table 2. (*continued*)

| Model | PSNR↑ | SSIM↑ | LPIPS↓ |
|---|---|---|---|
| Zero-DCE [9] | 22.12 | 0.8836 | 0.1003 |
| FDCE-Net [13] | 23.58 | 0.9216 | 0.0820 |
| UIE-DM [14] | 22.99 | 0.9024 | 0.0860 |
| AC-Net(ours) | **23.88** | **0.9263** | **0.0676** |

As shown in Table 2, AC-Net achieves the best performance in PSNR, SSIM, and LPIPS quality indicators, significantly out performing advanced methods such as UIE-DM, Zero DCE, and UIE-DM. The enhanced images exhibit higher image structure quality and better visual perception effects. The images in the UIEB dataset commonly suffer from color distortion, insufficient contrast, and structural blurring, which pose higher requirements for the adaptability of enhancement algorithms. AC-Net maintains stable and superior performance in this complex scenario, further demonstrating its robustness and generalization ability under cross domain conditions.This adaptability across scenes is of great significance in practical applications, especially in underwater imaging, night monitoring, robot vision and other fields where extreme illumination orimage degradation problems exist. AC-Net can provide reliable solutions for high-quality image enhancement, fully proving the progressiveness and practical value of this method.

### 3.5 Ablation Experiment

To verify the improvement performance of AESM and FEMB (Feature Extraction Module Based on Smooth Nonlinear Activation Mapping) on the original model, ablation experiments were conducted. The results of image enhancement are shown in Fig. 3, and the evaluation indicators are shown in Table 3. Among them, A is the benchmark model Zero-DCE, B is the benchmark model + FEMB, C is the benchmark model + AESM, and D is the AC-Net in this article.

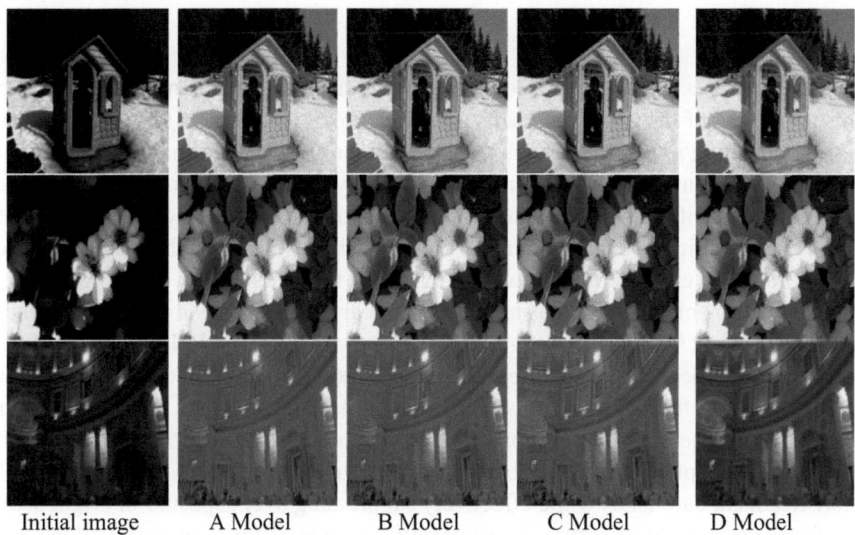

Initial image   A Model   B Model   C Model   D Model

**Fig. 3.** Comparison of AC-Net ablation experimental results

**Table 3.** Comparison of Evaluation Index Results for MHAC Net Ablation Experiment

| Model | AESM | FEMB | PSNR↑ | SSIM↑ | LPIPS↓ |
|---|---|---|---|---|---|
| A | NO | NO | 21.42 | 0.8393 | 0.1260 |
| B | NO | YES | 22.74 | 0.8420 | 0.1270 |
| C | YES | NO | 21.93 | 0.8517 | 0.1199 |
| D(AC-Net) | YES | YES | **23.95** | **0.8611** | **0.1116** |

As shown in Fig. 3, after ablation experiment comparison, the benchmark model Zero DCE (A) exhibits significant brightness unevenness and detail loss, while the (B) model has improved local contrast but still has some residual noise; (C) The model details are clearer; (D) Visually the best performance, with natural overall brightness, rich details, and distinct contrast levels.

The objective evaluation indicators for ablation experiments are shown in Table 3, with the optimal results displayed in bold. AC-Net (D) achieved the highest values in PSNR and SSIM, indicating that the enhanced image has the best quality and good structural preservation. At the same time, LPIPS was the lowest, indicating that the enhanced image is closer to human perception in terms of color and texture. Overall, the AC-Net proposed in this article outperforms other models in both visual and quantitative metrics, verifying the positive contribution of each submodule to low light image enhancement.

## 4 Summary

This article focuses on two key issues in low light image enhancement tasks: firstly, the non smoothness of the traditional activation function ReLU and its tendency to cause gradient vanishing in extremely dark areas, which limits the performance of the model in detail restoration and lighting transition; Secondly, the fixed step recursive enhancement method is difficult to adapt to complex lighting conditions, which can lead to excessive or insufficient enhancement.To solve the above problems, this paper proposes a low light image enhancement network AC-Net, which includes two core modules: a feature extraction module based on smooth nonlinear mapping and an adaptive enhancement step module. The former uses Softplus function instead of ReLU, and combines U-Net encoding decoding structure and shallow reconstruction mechanism to obtain smoother lighting transition, more stable gradient propagation, and finer local feature reconstruction; The latter uses global illumination modeling and probability sampling mechanism to adaptively predict the enhancement step size,enabling the model to fully restore details in dark areas while effectively suppressing over exposure in bright areas. The effectiveness of AC-Net was experimentally verified: in terms of visual effects, this method out performs existing methods in brightness transition, color reproduction, noise suppression, and high-frequency detail preservation; In terms of quantitative indicators, AC-Net achieved the best performance in PSNR, SSIM, and LPIPS on the LOLv2 public benchmark dataset, significantly surpassing mainstream models such as Zero DCE. It also shows stability in complex cross domain scenarios such as the UIEB underwater image dataset, verifying its good generalization ability. The ablation experiment further proves the key role of each module in performance improvement.This provides a new research direction for cross domain applications under low light conditions and collaborative optimization with high-level visual tasks.

**Acknowledgments.** This study was funded by National Natural Science Foundation of China (Grant number 62176273).

## References

1. Land, E.H.: The Retinex theory of color vision. Scientific American **237**(6), 108 (1977)
2. Guo, X., Li, Y., Ling, H.: LIME: low-light image enhancement via illumination map estimation. IEEE Trans. Image Process. **26**(2), 982–993 (2016)
3. Lore, K.G., Akintayo, A., Sarkar, S.: LLNet: a deep autoencoder approach to natural low-light image enhancement. Pattern Recognit. **61**, 650–662 (2017)
4. Yang, W., Wang, W., Huang, H., Wang, S., Liu, J.: Sparse gradient regularized deep retinex network for robust low-light image enhancement. IEEE Trans. Image Process. **30**, 2072–2086 (2021)
5. Guo, C., et al.: Zero-reference deep curve estimation for low-light image enhancement. In: Proceedings of the IEEE/CVF Conference on Computer Vision and Pattern Recognition, CVPR, pp.1780–1789 (2020)
6. Li, C., Guo, C., Loy, C.C.: Learning to enhance low-light image via zero-reference deep curve estimation. IEEE Trans. Pattern Anal. Mach. Intell. **44**(8), 4225–4238 (2021)

7. Liang, Z., Wang, Y., Ding, X., et al.: Single underwater image enhancement by attenuation map guided color correction and detail preserved dehazing. Neurocomputing **425**, 160–172 (2021)
8. Zhang, W., Wang, Y., Li, C.: Underwater image enhancement by attenuated color channel correction and detail preserved contrast enhancement. IEEE J. Oceanic Eng. **47**(3), 718–735 (2022)
9. Guo, C., Li, C., Guo, J., et al.: Zero-Reference Deep Curve Estimation for Low-Light Image Enhancement (2020)
10. Jiang, Y., Gong, X., Liu, D., et al.: Enlightengan: Deep light enhancement without paired supervision. IEEE Trans. Image Process. **30**, 2340–2349 (2021)
11. Lv, X., Dong, X., Jin, Z., et al.: L2dm: a diffusion model for low-light image enhancement. In: Chinese Conference on Pattern Recognition and Computer Vision (PRCV). Springer Nature Singapore, Singapore, pp. 130–145 (2023)
12. Cai, Y., Bian, H., Lin, J., et al.: Retinexformer: one-stage retinex-based transformer for low-light image enhancement. In: Proceedings of the IEEE/CVF International Conference on Computer Vision, pp. 12504–12513 (2023)
13. Cheng, Z., Fan, G., Zhou, J., et al.: FDCE-Net: underwater image enhancement with embedding frequency and dual color encoder. IEEE Transactions on Circuits and Systems for Video Technology (2024)
14. Tang, Y., Kawasaki, H., Iwaguchi, T.: Underwater image enhancement by transformer-based diffusion model with non-uniform sampling for skip strategy. In: ACM International Conference on Multimedia, pp. 5419–5427 (2023)

# Semi-supervised Scene Text Detection based on Teacher-Student Scheme and Cascaded Hybrid Network

Fuchen Ma, Songliang Guo, Xinfu Liu, and Yirui Wu[✉]

School of Computer Science and Software Engineering, Hohai University,
Nanjing 210093, China
wuyirui@hhu.edu.cn

**Abstract.** Scene text detection aims to accurately localize text instances in natural scenes. With impressive capability of deep learning methods, the related knowledge-based computer vision systems have achieved remarkable detection results in real-world scenarios. However, they generally require a large amount of training samples with huge manually labeling cost to extract sufficient vision knowledge. To address this problem, we propose a teacherstudent network for semi-supervised scene text detection. Specifically, we enhance which not only enhances knowledge learned by teacher network with pseudo-labeling enlarged training dataset, but also , which generates pseudo-labels through the teacher network and enlarge training dataset with pseudo-labeled samples, and then trains student network for detection with the enhanced dataset. The proposed method not only involves a pseudo-label quality assessment mechanism to improve the robustness of teacher network, but also designs a cascade hybrid framework in student network for informative information refinement. Experimental results demonstrate that our method achieves state-of-the-art performance on horizontal datasets (ICDAR2013), multi-oriented datasets (ICDAR2015), multilingual datasets (ICDAR2017-MLT) and arbitrary shape datasets (CTW1500, Total-Text).

**Keywords:** semi-supervised learning · scene text detection · teacher-student scheme · cascaded hybrid network.

## 1 Introduction

Scene text detection, critical for applications such as auto-driving [1] and document analysis [2], has advanced with deep learning [3]. However, its reliance on expensive labeled data limits generalization performance.

Facing insufficient data, previous methods[4–7] mainly use data augmentation with simple geometric and color transformations to create new instances. However, this provides insufficient data volume improvement. Additionally, annotation granularity varies between datasets and different annotation methods increase the volume of training data.

To enlarge data volume and improve generalization performance, we propose a semi-supervised scene text detection method based on a teacher-student scheme and cascaded hybrid network, the teacher network can generate pseudo-labels for unlabeled data, and the student network can train with pseudo-labels and labeled data. In order to generate high-quality pseudo-labels and improve the robustness of the network, we propose a pseudo-label quality evaluation mechanism that evaluates the importance scores of different pseudo-labels in the classification and regression subtasks.

Inspired by instance segmentation for arbitrary-shaped text detection, we design a cascaded hybrid architecture to refine detection results. Our method integrates text region classification, rectangular box generation, and text instance segmentation. To enhance multi-task consistency, we incorporate semantic segmentation branches for improved text-background differentiation and increase information flow bandwidth between subtasks, enabling collaborative training and improved detection coherence. The main contributions are:

- We propose a semi-supervised text detection method based on a teacher-student scheme that can generate pseudo-labels for unlabeled data to increase the size of the training dataset.
- We design a cascaded hybrid framework that can enable collaborative training between different subtasks and improve information bandwidth on text detection subtasks.
- A pseudo-label quality evaluation mechanism is designed to measure the quality of pseudo-labels, which improves the robustness of the student network for classification and regression subtasks.

## 2 Related Work

### 2.1 Text Detection Methods

Early scene text detection methods primarily identified individual characters for word assembly. Jaderberg et al. [8] generated word proposals, filtered them via random forests, and refined with regression. Recent advances in deep neural networks have significantly advanced the field. Current deep learning-based methods fall into two categories: bounding box regression-based and semantic segmentation-based approaches [9–11].

In object detection, bounding box regression-based methods employ manually set anchor boxes for text line classification and regression. For horizontal text detection, Tian et al. proposed CTPN [12], which predicts fixed-width text segments on vertical anchors and connects them via a BiLSTM. Liao et al. developed TextBoxes [13] based on SSD by redesigning anchor boxes and convolution kernels to better suit text detection, improving both accuracy and speed. To handle oriented text, they further introduced TextBoxes++ [14], which incorporates rotation angle prediction.

Semantic segmentation-based methods typically use FCN [15] to separate text and non-text regions, then apply post-processing to form text lines. Zhang et al.

[16] proposed a rule-based method combining FCN segmentation with MSER for character extraction and connection. Lyu et al. [17] integrated both regression and segmentation by transforming detection into a corner regression task, generating quadrilateral text lines through point detection and matching. Later, Long et al. [18] presented TextSnake, which represents text using disks along a centerline, though its complex representation requires multiple post-processing steps.

To sum up, although the above methods perform well in text detection, they still require quantity of samples to generate the distinguish visual features, making it difficult to detect texts with insufficient samples.

### 2.2 Semi-supervised learning

Since assigning labels for samples is often expensive, the idea of semi-supervised learning arises to train the learning model with both labeled and unlabeled data. Semi-supervised learning can greatly expand the amount of data and effectively improve the generalization performance of the network. The existing semi-supervised learning can be roughly divided into consistency learning-based methods [19–21] and pseudo-labeling-based method [22–24].

The consistency learning-based methods encourage a model's prediction to be similar with different views on the same input [25]. For example, Berthelot et al. [26] propose the MixMatch method, which first predicts low-entropy labels for data-augmented unlabeled examples, and then mixes labeled and unlabeled data using MixUp method. To exploit the importance of pre-trained weights in semi-supervised learning, Abuduweili et al. [20] introduce an adaptive consistency regularization. The pseudo-labeling-based methods usually build on a Teacher-Student architecture [27] to transform knowledge learned from the labeled to the unlabeled data. Believing that similar examples should get the same prediction, Iscen et al. [28] propose a transductive label propagation method, which builds on the manifold assumption to generate pseudo-labels for the unlabeled data. Sohn et al. [21] propose the FixMatch method, which first generates pseudo-labels by predicting weakly-augmented unlabeled images with the initially trained model, and then trains to predict the pseudo-labels by feeding a strongly-augmented dataset of the same images.

## 3 The Proposed Method

### 3.1 Network Overview

To address data scarcity in scene text detection, we propose a semi-supervised scene text detection method based on the teacher-student scheme. Let $\mathcal{I}_l = \{I_l^1, I_l^2, \ldots, I_l^{N_l}\}$ denote the labeled sample set and $\mathcal{I}_u = \{I_u^1, I_u^2, \ldots, I_u^{N_u}\}$ denote the unlabeled sample set, where $N_l$ and $N_u$ are the number of labeled and unlabeled data, respectively. The teacher network generates the pseudo-label set $g_{cls}$ on the $i$-th unlabeled data $I_u^i \in \mathcal{I}_u$, then the student network predicts on the enhanced data set containing $I_u^i$ and the unlabeled data with pseudo-labels.

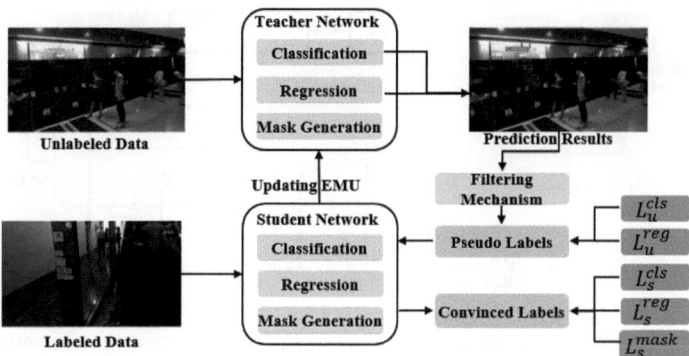

**Fig. 1.** Workflow of our method with two sub-networks: teacher and student networks. The teacher network generates the pseudo-labels, and the student network is trained on both labeled and unlabeled data. $L_s^{cls}$, $L_s^{reg}$, $L_s^{mask}$ denote the classification, regression, and mask losses on labeled data, respectively, and $L_u^{cls}$, $L_u^{reg}$ denote the classification and regression loss on unlabeled data, respectively.

The workflow of our method is shown in Fig. 1. There are two branches of pseudo-labels for the student network to train, one for classification and the other for regression. According to the consistency regularization principle of semi-supervised learning [29], slight noise in the data could improve the performance of the model. Therefore, different noises are added to the data from the teacher and student networks.

Inspired by the hybrid task cascade R-CNN [30] which progressively learns and integrates discriminative features, we propose a Text Context Fusion and Segmentation (TCFS) module to integrate the spatial context information generated by the semantic segmentation branch into the detection and regression tasks at each stage.

As shown in Fig. 2, the FPN [31] backbone extracts multi-scale feature maps, followed by RPN generating candidate boxes. RoIAlign then extracts task-specific features for subsequent classification and regression tasks. The TCFS module generates semantic segmentation maps infused with contextual spatial information to bridge task representations. Instance segmentation integrates semantic outputs with detection results, while non-maximum suppression [32] eliminates redundant boxes from anchor-rich outputs.

Essentially, the teacher-student scheme can be trained on either labeled or unlabeled data. During each iteration, a training data batch is formed by sampling both labeled and unlabeled data at a given sampling rate $S_r$. For the input image, the teacher network first weakly amplifies it, then the student network predicts it using the strongly amplifying method. Based on the above discussion, the overall loss function can be written as:

$$L = L_s + \alpha \cdot L_u, \tag{1}$$

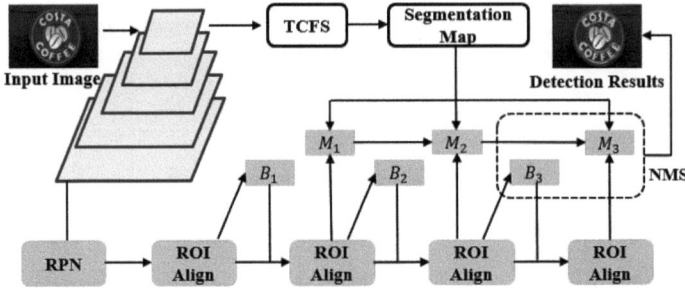

**Fig. 2.** Structure design of the proposed network. TCFS generates the semantic segmentation feature map, and can enhance the detecting performance of text instances with additional and useful information. $B_t$ and $M_t$ ($t = 1, 2, 3$) are the bounding box header and segmentation header, respectively.

where $L_s$ is the supervised loss on labeled data, $L_u$ is the unsupervised loss on unlabeled data, and $\alpha$ is a hyper-parameter. Let $L_{cls}$, $L_{reg}$, $L_{mask}$, and $L_{seg}$ denote the classification, regression, mask, and semantic segmentation loss, respectively. Thus, $L_s$ and $L_u$ can be normalized as

$$L_s = \frac{1}{N_l} \sum_{i=1}^{N_l} \left( L_{cls}\left(I_l^i\right) + L_{reg}\left(I_l^i\right) + L_{mask}\left(I_l^i\right) \right) + L_{seg},$$

$$L_u = \frac{1}{N_u} \sum_{i=1}^{N_u} \left( L_{cls}\left(I_u^i\right) + L_{reg}\left(I_u^i\right) \right), \qquad (2)$$

where $I_l^i \in \mathcal{I}_l$ and $I_u^i \in \mathcal{I}_u$ denote the $i$-th labeled and unlabeled data, respectively. Due to the low quality of masks generated by the teacher network on $\mathcal{I}_u$, the mask loss is calculated only on $\mathcal{I}_l$.

### 3.2 Multi-stage Cascade Network

We propose a multi-stage cascade network for text detection, where input information from border calibration, text area classification, and text instance segmentation are fused and optimized. Assuming that $x$ is the feature map obtained from the backbone network, the feature map of the bounding box and RoI at the $t$-th stage can be denoted as $x_t^{box}$ and $x_t^{mask}$. Let $r_t$ and $m_t$ represent the results of box detection and mask segmentation at the $t$-th stage, respectively. We generate the feature map of the detected bounding box $x_t^{box}$ and mask $x_t^{mask}$ by

$$x_t^{box} = P(x, r_{t-1}) + P(S(x), r_{t-1}), \qquad (3)$$
$$x_t^{mask} = P(x, r_t) + P(S(x), r_t), \qquad (4)$$

where $P(x, r_{t-1}), P(x, r_t)$ mean the RoI pooling operation on $x$ at the $t-1$ stage and the $t$ stage, respectively, and $S(x)$ means the semantic segmentation operation of TCFS on $x$.

Since the generated feature map considers the feature information from the backbone and semantic segmentation, $r_t$ and $m_t$ can be calculated by

$$r_t = B_t\left(x_t^{box}\right), \tag{5}$$

$$m_t = M_t\left(F(x_t^{mask}, m_{t-1}^-)\right), \tag{6}$$

where $B_t(\cdot)$ and $M_t(\cdot)$ denote the bounding box header and segmentation header at the $t$-th stage, respectively. In (6), $F(\cdot, \cdot)$ fuses the feature maps of the current and previous stages, and $m_{t-1}^-$ is the intermediate feature of $M_{t-1}(\cdot)$.

In bounding box prediction, the computation is jointly determined by the detected bounding boxes of the previous stages and the feature maps in backbone network. Therefore, we design the overall structure $F(\cdot, \cdot)$ for multi-stage feature map fusion. Let $m_{t-1}^-$ also be the output feature map before the inverse convolution operation at the $t-1$-th stage and $C_t(\cdot)$ denote the convolution operation that aligns with $x_t^{mask}$. $F(\cdot, \cdot)$ can be formulated as

$$F\left(x_t^{mask}, m_{t-1}^-\right) = x_t^{mask} + C_t\left(m_{t-1}^-\right). \tag{7}$$

Therefore, the generation of $m_{t-1}^-$ can be written as

$$\begin{cases} m_1^- = M_1^-\left(x_t^{mask}\right), \\ m_2^- = M_2^-\left(F\left(x_t^{mask}, m_1^-\right)\right), \\ \ldots, \\ m_{t-1}^- = M_t^-\left(F\left(x_t^{mask}, m_{t-2}^-\right)\right), \end{cases} \tag{8}$$

where $M_t^-(\cdot)$ denotes the eigen transforms with respect to $M_t(\cdot)$.

## 3.3 Text Context Fusion and Segmentation Module

As explained in Sect. 3.1, the Text Context Fusion and Segmentation (TCFS) module generates semantic segmentation maps from multi-scale FPN feature inputs, enhancing accuracy for classification, bounding box regression, and text instance segmentation. As shown in Fig. 3, TCFS first aligns all feature layers to the 4th FPN layer's downsampled size (4×). Smaller feature maps undergo channel alignment via 1×1 convolution, followed by 2× upsampling and refinement with 3×3 convolution before element-wise summation. Larger maps (e.g., layer 5) are downsampled and refined with 3×3 convolution to integrate multi-scale contexts. The obtained feature map is further refined by a 3 × 3 convolution layer, thus incorporating multi-scale feature information after all these operations.

To obtain contextual information from the generated feature map, the feature map is fed into an attention structure, which allows to focus on key regions and improve its ability to discriminate between textual regions and background areas. Finally, semantic segmentation feature maps and results are generated.

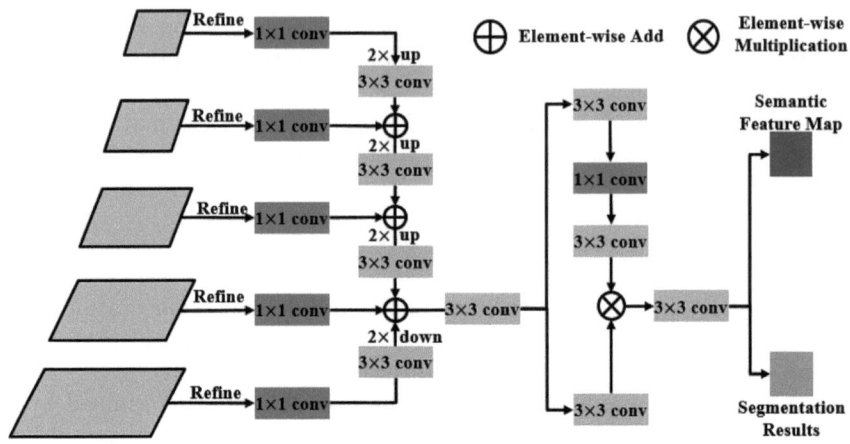

**Fig. 3.** Structure design of TCFS module.

### 3.4 Pseudo-Label Generation Mechanism

The quality of the pseudo-labels plays a crucial role in training, as a large number of redundancies are generated in order to pursue high-quality pseudo-labels for training. Although a large number of redundant outputs have been filtered out by non-maximum suppression, there are still a large number of low quality results, which will lead to a decrease in detection accuracy.

To ensure high-quality pseudo-labels, we propose a pseudo-label generation mechanism with the structure shown in Fig. 4. Since classification and regression tasks differ, we design separate classification filtering and regression filtering mechanisms. This mechanism evaluates pseudo-labels generated by the teacher network to obtain their task-specific reliability.

**Classification Filtering Mechanism.** First, the input images are weakly and strongly enhanced, with the enhanced results are then fed into the teacher-student scheme to generate bounding boxes. As a supervised teacher network, the output of the student network is divided into positive and negative samples, thus obtaining the probability $r$ to be considered as text regions. The generated pseudo-label would only participate in training if $r$ is greater than a certain threshold, i.e., 0.8.

To classify the textual and non-textual regions, all negative samples on unlabeled data are still weighted to improve the capbality to distinguish text from background. Let the set of detected boxes $\{b_i^{text}\}$ be the text regions and the set of detected boxes $\{b_i^{bg}\}$ be the background regions. The loss function $L_u^{cls}$ on the unlabeled dataset for classification is formulated as

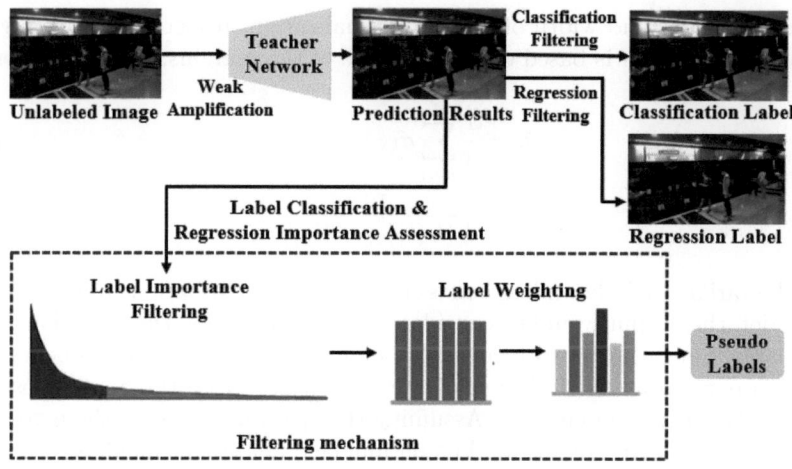

**Fig. 4.** Structure design of our pseudo-label generation mechanism.

$$L_u^{cls} = \frac{1}{N_b^{fg}} \sum_{i=1}^{N_b^{text}} l_{cls}\left(b_i^{text}, g_{cls}\right)$$
$$+ \sum_{j=1}^{N_b^{bg}} w_j \cdot l_{cls}\left(b_j^{bg}, g_{cls}\right), \quad (9)$$

where the weight $w_j = \frac{1}{\sum_{k=1}^{N_b^{text}} r_k} \cdot r_j$. In (9), $g_{cls}$ is the pseudo-labels generated by the teacher network for the classification task, and $l_{cls}$ is the edge classification loss. $N_b^{text}$ and $N_b^{bg}$ denote the detection box number contained in $\{b_i^{text}\}$ and $\{b_i^{bg}\}$, respectively. $r_j$ denotes the probability that the $j$-th detection box is judged as a background region.

**Regression filtering mechanism.** Regression and classification are different tasks, the classification score cannot be used as a basis for regression labeling, which requires the reliability of regression to be assessed in a different way.

If two samples are similar in the input space, their labels should also be similar in semantic space. Following such a smoothing assumption, we propose consistency-based regression reliability estimation. Defining the pseudo-label candidate box generated by the teacher network as $b_i$, a perturbation is first applied to $b_i$, and then the perturbed border is fed into the teacher network to obtain a fine-tuned new border. Let $\hat{b}_i$ be the new border obtained by re-feeding the teacher network after applying the perturbation. By repeating above steps, we have a set of fine-tuned edges $\{\hat{b}_{i,j}\}$, where $\hat{b}_{i,j}$ is the border after the $j$-th perturbation.

For the $k$-th coordinate, let $\sigma_k$ denote the standard deviation of $\{\hat{b}_{i,j}\}$ and $\hat{\sigma}_k$ denote the standard deviation of $\{\hat{b}_{i,j}\}$ in the perturbed set. $h(b_i)$ and $w(b_i)$

denote the height and width of $b_i$ after normalization, respectively. The regression reliability which is based on the variance of the margins, can be written as

$$\bar{\sigma}_i = \frac{1}{4}\sum_{k=1}^{4} \hat{\sigma}_k, \tag{10}$$

$$\hat{\sigma}_k = \frac{\sigma_k}{\frac{1}{2}\left(h\left(b_i\right) + w\left(b_i\right)\right)}. \tag{11}$$

If the variance of a bounding box is smaller after perturbations to re-calibrate the border, the output would be considered as consistent and the detection boxes are reliable. Since the network generates a large number of detection boxes, the computational cost is high. We calculate the variance to estimate the possibility of the latter pseudo-labeling. Assuming that pseudo-labels for the regression is denoted as $g_{reg}$, the regression loss on unlabeled data is defined as

$$L_u^{reg} = \frac{1}{N_b^{text}} \sum_{i=1}^{N_b^{text}} \sigma_i \cdot L_{reg}\left(b_i^{text}, g_{reg}\right), \tag{12}$$

where $b_i^{text}$ denotes the $i$-th box designated as the text region, and $N_b^{text}$ denotes the number of text regions. $\sigma_i$ denotes the variance after border perturbation for the $i$-th prediction result.

## 4 Experiment

### 4.1 Datasets and Evaluation Metrics

We consider five public, widely-used datasets for scene text detection, i.e., ICDAR2013 [33], ICDAR2015 [34], ICDAR2017-MLT [35], Total-Text [36], and CTW-1500 [36].Note that for both CTW-1500 and Total-Text, we use the training sets of them as their respective labeled data, and the other data as unlabeled data.

Following recent scene text recognition work[11,37], three evaluation metrics, namely Precision, Recall, and F1-score are employed.

### 4.2 Implementation Details

We use the weights pre-trained on MS-COCO as initial values for the whole network. In the text detection dataset, we use the SGD trainer with an initial learning rate of 0.01. Weight decay and momentum are set to $1e^{-4}$ and 0.9, respectively. For training on the ICDAR2013 and ICDAR2015 datasets, the sampling rate $S_r$ is set to 0.6 , for a total of 500 epochs of training. In the ICDAR2017-MLT dataset, the sampling rate $S_r$ is set to 0.4, for a total training of 400 epochs are trained. For training on the CTW-1500 and Total-Text datasets, the sampling rate $S_r$ is set to 0.5, for a total of 600 epochs of training.

**Table 1.** Comparisons on ICDAR2013 for horizontal scene text detection.

| Method | Precision | Recall | F1-score |
|---|---|---|---|
| CTPN [38] | 93.0 | 83.0 | 88.0 |
| SegLink [39] | 87.7 | 83.0 | 85.3 |
| TextBoxes [13] | 88.0 | 74.0 | 81.0 |
| DDR [40] | 92.0 | 81.0 | 86.0 |
| PixelLink [41] | 86.4 | 83.6 | 84.5 |
| PixelLink+MS [41] | 88.6 | 87.5 | 88.1 |
| SSTD [42] | 88.0 | 86.0 | 87.0 |
| WordSup [43] | 93.3 | 87.5 | 90.3 |
| RRD [44] | 88.0 | 75.0 | 81 |
| RRD+MS [44] | 92.0 | 86.0 | 89.0 |
| Mask R-CNN [37] | 91.5 | 89.2 | 90.2 |
| Ours | **94.5** | **91.4** | **92.9** |

**Table 2.** Comparisons on ICDAR2015 for arbitrary orientation based-scene text detection.

| Method | Precision | Recall | F1-score |
|---|---|---|---|
| CTPN [38] | 74.2 | 51.6 | 60.9 |
| SegLink [39] | 73.1 | 76.8 | 75.0 |
| DDR [40] | 82.0 | 80.0 | 81.0 |
| PixelLink [41] | 82.0 | 85.5 | 83.7 |
| SSTD [42] | 80.0 | 73.0 | 77.0 |
| East [45] | 73.4 | 83.5 | 78.2 |
| FCE [46] | 85.1 | **84.2** | 84.6 |
| RRD [44] | 79.0 | 85.6 | 82.2 |
| Mask R-CNN [37] | 85.7 | 78.5 | 81.9 |
| Ours | **88.4** | 82.2 | **85.2** |

In the comparison supervised learning method, the initial learning rate of 0.01 is used in all datasets, 400 epochs are trained on the ICDAR 2013 dataset, and 200 epochs are uniformly trained on the other datasets.

The experiments are conducted on 4 Tesla V100s with a batch size of 4 per GPU. The operating system is Ubuntu 18.04, and pytorch is used as the deep learning framework. Our method is built on MMdetection and MMOCR environment.

### 4.3 Comparisons with State-of-the-art Methods

**Horizontal Scene Text Detection.** As shown in Table1, the proposed method achieves the best performance on the ICDAR2013 dataset, outperforming the second-best by 1.2% in precision, 2.2% in recall, and 2.6% in F1-score, which demonstrates the effectiveness of the cascaded hybrid network.

**Table 3.** Comparisons on ICDAR2017-MLT for multilingual text detection.

| Method | Precision | Recall | F1-score |
|---|---|---|---|
| He et al. [47] | 76.7 | 57.9 | 66.0 |
| Liao et al. [48] | **83.8** | 55.6 | 66.8 |
| PSENet [49] | 73.7 | 68.2 | 70.8 |
| LOMO [36] | 78.8 | 60.6 | 68.5 |
| CRAFT [50] | 80.6 | 68.2 | 73.9 |
| Mask R-CNN [37] | 77.4 | 70.5 | 73.8 |
| Ours | 80.7 | **73.9** | **77.1** |

**Table 4.** Comparisons on the CTW-1500 and Total-Text datasets for arbitrary shape text detection.

| Method | CTW-1500 | | |
|---|---|---|---|
| | Precision | Recall | F1-score |
| CTD+TLOC [51] | 77.4 | 69.8 | 73.4 |
| TextSnake [18] | 67.9 | **85.3** | 75.6 |
| PSENet [49] | 80.6 | 75.6 | 78.0 |
| EAST [45] | 78.7 | 49.1 | 60.4 |
| FCE [46] | **85.7** | 80.7 | 83.1 |
| TextRay [52] | 82.8 | 80.4 | 81.6 |
| LOMO [36] | **85.7** | 76.5 | 80.8 |
| CSE [53] | 81.0 | 76.0 | 78.4 |
| Mask R-CNN [37] | 80.2 | 82.9 | 81.5 |
| Ours | 83.6 | 84.7 | **84.1** |
| Method | Total-Text | | |
| | Precision | Recall | F1-score |
| SegLink [39] | 30.0 | 23.8 | 26.7 |
| East [45] | 50.0 | 36.2 | 42.0 |
| TextSnake [18] | 82.7 | 74.5 | 78.4 |
| CSE [53] | 81.4 | 79.1 | 80.2 |
| TextDragon [54] | **85.6** | 75.7 | 80.3 |
| PSENet [49] | 84.0 | 77.9 | 80.9 |
| TextRay [52] | 83.5 | 77.9 | 80.6 |
| Mask R-CNN [37] | 80.5 | 79.5 | 80.0 |
| Ours | 82.8 | **84.0** | **83.4** |

**Scene Text Detection in Arbitrary Orientation.** Table 2 shows the experimental results on the ICDAR2015 dataset for arbitrary orientation based-scene text detection. For precision and F1-score, our method outperforms the

**Table 5.** Ablation studies on the ICDAR2017-MLT dataset.

| Method | Precision | Recall | F1-score |
|---|---|---|---|
| Mask R-CNN | 77.4 | 70.5 | 73.8 |
| Cascade Mask R-CNN | 77.9 | 71.2 | 74.4 |
| Supervised learning | 78.6 | 71.6 | 74.9 |
| Ours | **80.7** | **73.9** | **77.1** |

**Table 6.** Model performance analyses about few-shot learning on ICDAR2017-MLT dataset with 20% of labeling and on CTW-1500 dataset.

| Method | ICDAR2017-MLT | | |
|---|---|---|---|
| | Precision | Recall | F1-score |
| Supervised learning | 68.5 | 57.3 | 62.4 |
| Ours | **78.6** | **64.3** | **70.7** |
| Method | CTW-1500 | | |
| | Precision | Recall | F1-score |
| Masked pseudo-labeling | **83.7** | 84.6 | **84.1** |
| Ours | 83.6 | **84.7** | **84.1** |

state-of-the-art by 0.3 and 0.2, respectively. For recall, our method is slightly inferior to several comparative methods. This is because some images in ICDAR2015 are blurred with a lot of small text, which makes the detection much more difficult.

**Multilingual Text Detection.** As shown in Table 3, on the multilingual ICDAR2017-MLT dataset, the proposed method achieves competitive precision, second only to [48]. Its effective use of unlabeled data enhances generalization, making it more suitable for complex multilingual text detection.

**Arbitrary Shape Text Detection.** As shown in Table 4, the proposed method achieves competitive performance on CTW-1500 and Total-Text datasets, delivering significant F1-scores. While its precision is slightly inferior to a few specialized methods, the integrated design of multi-stage information flow and joint task training enhances its capability in detecting multi-directional and curved text.

### 4.4 Ablation Studies

We perform a set of ablation experiments on the ICDAR2017-MLT dataset to verify the effectiveness of our design. In Table 5, "Mask R-CNN" serves as the baseline method, "Cascade Mask R-CNN" means the model with multi-stage cascade design, and "Supervised learning" adds semantic segmentation branch on the basis of Cascade Mask R-CNN. The multi-stage cascade structure and semantic segmentation branch significantly improve performance over the Mask R-CNN baseline. Furthermore, the scheme effectively leverages unlabeled data, enhancing generalization in multilingual scenarios while reducing annotation cost.

### 4.5 Model Performance Analysis on Few-shot Learning

As shown in Table 6, our method demonstrates strong few-shot learning capabilities. Under the 20% labeled data setting on ICDAR2017-MLT, our teacher-student scheme significantly outperforms supervised learning, achieving F1-scores close to fully-supervised methods. On CTW-1500, our approach achieves the best F1-score, demonstrating that the semantic segmentation branch effectively improves text instance segmentation accuracy in complex scenes (Table 6).

## 5 Conclusions

We propose a semi-supervised scene text detection method using a cascaded hybrid network with a teacher-student scheme. It incorporates classification and regression filtering mechanisms to generate high-quality pseudo-labels from unlabeled data. The multi-stage design with a semantic segmentation branch enhances information flow and inter-task collaboration. Experiments demonstrate its effectiveness, particularly in low-resource labeled data scenarios.

**Acknowledgments.** This study was in part supported by the National Key R&D Program of China (No. 2023YFC3006501); Natural Science Foundation of Jiangsu Province of China (No. BK20242050); and High Performance Computing Platform, Hohai University.

## References

1. Ando, A., Gidaris, S., Bursuc, A., Puy, G., Boulch, A., Marlet, R.: RangeViT: towards vision transformers for 3D semantic segmentation in autonomous driving. In: Proceedings of IEEE Conference on Computer Vision and Pattern Recognition, pp. 5240–5250 (2023)
2. Aralikatte, R., Abdou, M., Lent, H.C., Hershcovich, D., Sgaard, A.: Joint semantic analysis with document-level cross-task coherence rewards. In: Proceedings of AAAI Conference on Artificial Intelligence, pp. 12516–12525 (2021)
3. Su, Y., et al.: LRANet: towards accurate and efficient scene text detection with low-rank approximation network, pp. 4979–4987. AAAI Press (2024)
4. Wang, C.Y., Bochkovskiy, A., Liao, H.Y.M.: YOLOv7: trainable bag-of-freebies sets new state-of-the-art for real-time object detectors. In: Proceedings of The IEEE Conference on Computer Vision and Pattern Recognition, pp. 7464–7475 (2023)

5. Axelrod, B., Garg, S., Sharan, V., Valiant, G.: Sample Amplification: increasing dataset size even when learning is impossible. In: Proceedings of International Conference on Machine Learning, pp. 442–451 (2020)
6. Hao, Y., Orlitsky, A.: Data Amplification: instance-optimal property estimation. In: Proceedings of International Conference on Machine Learning, pp. 4049–4059 (2020)
7. Yu, W., Liu, Y., Zhu, X., Cao, H., Sun, X., Bai, X.: Turning a CLIP model into a scene text spotter. IEEE Trans. Pattern Anal. Mach. Intell. **46**(9), 6040–6054 (2024)
8. Jaderberg, M., Simonyan, K., Vedaldi, A., Zisserman, A.: Reading text in the wild with convolutional neural networks. Int. J. Comput. Vision **116**, 1–20 (2016)
9. Duan, C., Fu, P., Guo, S., Jiang, Q., Wei, X.: ODM: a text image further alignment pre-training approach for scene text detection and spotting. In: IEEE/CVF Conference on Computer Vision and Pattern Recognition, CVPR, pp. 15587–15597. IEEE (2024)
10. Zheng, J., Fan, H., Zhang, L.: Kernel adaptive convolution for scene text detection via distance map prediction. In: IEEE/CVF Conference on Computer Vision and Pattern Recognition, CVPR 2024, Seattle, WA, USA, June 16-22, 2024, pp. 5957–5966. IEEE (2024)
11. Xue, C., Huang, J., Zhang, W., Lu, S., Wang, C., Bai, S.: Image-to-character-to-word transformers for accurate scene text recognition. IEEE Trans. Pattern Anal. Mach. Intell. **45**(11), 12908–12921 (2023)
12. Tian, Z., Huang, W., He, T., He, P., Qiao, Y.: Detecting text in natural image with connectionist text proposal network. In: Proceedings of European Conference on Computer Vision, pp. 56–72 (2016)
13. Liao, M., Shi, B., Bai, X., Wang, X., Liu, W.: Textboxes: a fast text detector with a single deep neural network. In: Proceedings of AAAI Conference on Artificial Intelligence, pp. 4161–4167 (2017)
14. Liao, M., Shi, B., Bai, X.: Textboxes++: a single-shot oriented scene text detector. IEEE Trans. Image Process. **27**(8), 3676–3690 (2018)
15. Yang, F., Li, X., Cheng, H., Guo, Y., Chen, L., Li, J.: Multi-scale bidirectional FCN for object skeleton extraction. In: Proceedings of AAAI Conference on Artificial Intelligence, pp. 7461–7468 (2018)
16. Zhang, D., Zhang, H., Li, H., Hu, X.: RR-FCN: rotational region-based fully convolutional networks for object detection. In: Proceedings of Engineering Applications of Neural Networks, pp. 58–70 (2018)
17. Lyu, P., Yang, Z., Leng, X., Wu, X., Li, R., Shen, X.: 2D attentional irregular scene text recognizer. CoRR **abs/1906.05708** (2019)
18. Long, S., Ruan, J., Zhang, W., He, X., Wu, W., Yao, C.: TextSnake: a flexible representation for detecting text of arbitrary shapes. In: Proceedings of European Conference on Computer Vision, pp. 19–35 (2018)
19. Miyato, T., ichi Maeda, S., Koyama, M., Ishii, S.: Virtual adversarial training: a regularization method for supervised and semi-supervised learning. IEEE Trans. Pattern Anal. Mach. Intell. **41**(8), 1979–1993 (2019)
20. Abuduweili, A., Li, X., Shi, H., Xu, C.Z., Dou, D.: Adaptive consistency regularization for semi-supervised transfer learning. In: IEEE Conference on Computer Vision and Pattern Recognition, pp. 6923–6932 (2021)
21. Sohn, K., et al.: FixMatch: simplifying semi-supervised learning with consistency and confidence. In: Proceedings of Conference on Neural Information Processing Systems (2020)

22. Xie, Q., Luong, M.T., Hovy, E.H., Le, Q.V.: Self-training with noisy student improves imagenet classification. In: Proceedings of IEEE Conference on Computer Vision and Pattern Recognition, pp. 10684–10695 (2020)
23. Xie, Q., Dai, Z., Hovy, E.H., Luong, T., Le, Q.: Unsupervised data augmentation for consistency training. In: Proceedings of Conference on Neural Information Processing Systems (2020)
24. Wang, Q., Li, W., Gool, L.V.: Semi-supervised learning by augmented distribution alignment. In: Proceedings of IEEE International Conference on Computer Vision, pp. 1466–1475 (2019)
25. Zhang, X., Wang, Z., Du, B.: Deep dynamic interest learning with session local and global consistency for click-through rate predictions. IEEE Trans. Ind. Info. **18**(5), 3306–3315 (2022)
26. Berthelot, D., Carlini, N., Goodfellow, I.J., Papernot, N., Oliver, A., Raffel, C.: MixMatch: a holistic approach to semi-supervised learning. In: Proceedings of Conference on Neural Information Processing Systems, pp. 5050–5060 (2019)
27. Huo, C., Jin, D., Li, Y., He, D., Yang, Y.B., Wu, L.: T2-GNN: graph neural networks for graphs with incomplete features and structure via teacher-student distillation. In: Proceedings of AAAI Conference on Artificial Intelligence, pp. 4339–4346 (2023)
28. Iscen, A., Tolias, G., Avrithis, Y., Chum, O.: Label propagation for deep semi-supervised learning. In: Proceedings of IEEE Conference on Computer Vision and Pattern Recognition, pp. 5070–5079 (2019)
29. Kim, J., et al.: Conmatch: Semi-supervised learning with confidence-guided consistency regularization. In: Proceedings of European Conference on Computer Vision, pp. 674–690 (2022)
30. Chen, K., et al.: Hybrid task cascade for instance segmentation. In: Proceedings of IEEE Conference on Computer Vision and Pattern Recognition, pp. 4974–4983 (2019)
31. Lin, T., Dollár, P., Girshick, R.B., He, K., Hariharan, B., Belongie, S.J.: Feature pyramid networks for object detection. In: 2017 IEEE Conference on Computer Vision and Pattern Recognition, CVPR 2017, Honolulu, HI, USA, July 21-26, 2017, pp. 936–944. IEEE Computer Society (2017)
32. Kitchen, L., Rosenfeld, A.: Non-maximum suppression of gradient magnitudes makes them easier to threshold. Pattern Recognit. Lett. **1**(2), 93–94 (1982)
33. Karatzas, D., et al.: ICDAR 2013 robust reading competition. In: Proceedings of International Conference on Document Analysis and Recognition, pp. 1484–1493 (2013)
34. Karatzas, D., et al.: ICDAR 2015 competition on robust reading. In: Proceedings of International Conference on Document Analysis and Recognition, pp. 1156–1160 (2015)
35. Nayef, N., et al.: ICDAR2017 robust reading challenge on multi-lingual scene text detection and script identification - RRC-MLT. In: Proceedings of International Conference on Document Analysis and Recognition, pp. 1454–1459 (2017)
36. Zhang, C., Liang, B., Huang, Z., En, M., Han, J., Ding, E., Ding, X.: Look more than once: an accurate detector for text of arbitrary shapes. In: Proceedings of IEEE Conference on Computer Vision and Pattern Recognition, pp. 10552–10561 (2019)
37. von Braun, M.S., Frenzel, P., ding, C.K., Fuchs, M.: Utilizing mask R-CNN for waterline detection in canoe sprint video analysis. In: Proceedings of IEEE Conference on Computer Vision and Pattern Recognition, pp. 3826–3835 (2020)

38. Zhang, B., Dong, J., Zhao, Z., Meng, Z., Su, F.: MT2: multi-task mean teacher for semi-supervised cell segmentation. In: Proceedings of Neural Information Processing Systems, pp. 1–13 (2022)
39. Shi, B., Bai, X., Belongie, S.J.: Detecting oriented text in natural images by linking segments. In: Proceedings of IEEE Conference on Computer Vision and Pattern Recognition, pp. 3482–3490 (2017)
40. He, W., Zhang, X.Y., Yin, F., Liu, C.L.: Deep direct regression for multi-oriented scene text detection. In: Proceedings of International Conference on Computer Vision, pp. 745–753 (2017)
41. Deng, D., Liu, H., Li, X., Cai, D.: PixelLink: detecting scene text via instance segmentation. In: Proceedings of AAAI Conference on Artificial Intelligence, pp. 6773–6780 (2018)
42. He, P., Huang, W., He, T., Zhu, Q., Qiao, Y., Li, X.: Single shot text detector with regional attention. In: Proceedings of International Conference on Computer Vision, pp. 3066–3074 (2017)
43. Hu, H., Zhang, C., Luo, Y., Wang, Y., Han, J., Ding, E.: WordSup: exploiting word annotations for character based text detection. In: Proceedings of International Conference on Computer Vision, pp. 4950–4959 (2017)
44. Liao, M., Zhu, Z., Shi, B., Xia, G.S., Bai, X.: Rotation-sensitive regression for oriented scene text detection. In: Proceedings of IEEE Conference on Computer Vision and Pattern Recognition, pp. 5909–5918 (2018)
45. Zhou, X., et al.: East: An efficient and accurate scene text detector. In: Proceedings of IEEE Conference on Computer Vision and Pattern Recognition, pp. 2642–2651 (2017)
46. Zhu, Y., Chen, J., Liang, L., Kuang, Z., Jin, L., Zhang, W.: Fourier contour embedding for arbitrary-shaped text detection. In: Proceedings of IEEE Conference on Computer Vision and Pattern Recognition, pp. 3123–3131 (2021)
47. He, W., Zhang, X.Y., Yin, F., Liu, C.L.: Multi-oriented and multi-lingual scene text detection with direct regression. IEEE Trans. Image Process. **27**(11), 5406–5419 (2018)
48. Liao, M., Lyu, P., He, M., Yao, C., Wu, W., Bai, X.: Mask TextSpotter: an end-to-end trainable neural network for spotting text with arbitrary shapes. IEEE Trans. Pattern Anal. Mach. Intell. **43**(2), 532–548 (2021)
49. Wang, W., Xie, E., Li, X., Hou, W., Lu, T., Yu, G., Shao, S.: Shape robust text detection with progressive scale expansion network. In: Proceedings of IEEE Conference on Computer Vision and Pattern Recognition. pp. 9336–9345 (2019)
50. Baek, Y., Lee, B., Han, D., Yun, S., Lee, H.: Character region awareness for text detection. In: Proceedings of IEEE Conference on Computer Vision and Pattern Recognition, pp. 9365–9374 (2019)
51. Liu, Y., Jin, L., Zhang, S., Zhang, S.: Detecting curve text in the wild: new dataset and new solution. CoRR **abs/1712.02170** (2017)
52. Wang, F., Chen, Y., Wu, F., Li, X.: TextRay: contour-based geometric modeling for arbitrary-shaped scene text detection. In: Proceedings of ACM Conference on Multimedia, pp. 111–119 (2020)
53. Liu, Z., Lin, G., Yang, S., Liu, F., Lin, W., Goh, W.L.: Towards robust curve text detection with conditional spatial expansion. In: Proceedings of IEEE Conference on Computer Vision and Pattern Recognition, pp. 7269–7278 (2019)
54. Feng, W., He, W., Yin, F., Zhang, X.Y., Liu, C.L.: TextDragon: an end-to-end framework for arbitrary shaped text spotting. In: Proceedings of International Conference on Computer Vision, pp. 9075–9084 (2019)

# Towards Fast-Slow Thinking in Conversational Emotion Recognition via Causal Prompting with Peak-End Rule

Ran Jing[1], Geng Tu[1], and Ruifeng Xu[1,2,3](✉)

[1] Harbin Institute of Technology, Shenzhen, China
{22b951011,24S051023}@stu.hit.edu.cn, xuruifeng@hit.edu.cn
[2] Peng Cheng Laboratory, Shenzhen, China
[3] GD Prov. Key Lab. of Novel Security Intelligence Technologies, Shenzhen, China

**Abstract.** The rapid advancement of large language models (LLMs) has opened new opportunities for Emotion Recognition in Conversation (ERC). However, most existing LLM-based approaches neglect two underlying causal relationships: when utterances drive emotions, and when emotions drive utterances. These two directions closely align with the dual-system theory in psychology, which distinguishes between fast and slow thinking. To explicitly model these bidirectional causal dynamics, we propose a Dynamic Causal-Prompted Framework (DCPF), which leverages causal prompting to enhance the contextual understanding of LLMs. Inspired by the Peak-End Rule, DCPF evaluates whether the current utterance reflects fast or slow thinking and infers its causal orientation accordingly. Based on this analysis, DCPF dynamically adjusts corresponding causal prompts at each iteration to guide the LLM in modelling conversational context more accurately. Experiments on multiple benchmarks demonstrate that DCPF significantly improves ERC performance, particularly in long-context scenarios, and proves effective in both multimodal and text-only ERC tasks.

**Keywords:** Conversational Emotion Recognition · Causal Prompting · Fast-Slow Thinking · Peak-End Rule

## 1 Introduction

Emotion recognition in conversations (ERC) aims to identify the emotion of each utterance in conversations. This task plays a crucial role in applications such as recommendation systems and dialogue generation [31,32]. With the rise of large language models (LLMs), their strong capabilities in contextual understanding have been increasingly leveraged in ERC [17].

Despite advances in LLM-based ERC, they neglect two underlying causal relationships: when utterances drive emotions, and when emotions drive utterances. These two directions are closely aligned with the dual-system theory in psychology, which distinguishes between fast and slow thinking [16]. Specifically, emotion can affect the use of language [1], indicating a more reactive, fast-thinking mode; conversely, language can be the cause of emotion [26], reflecting a deliberative, slow-thinking process on the part of the speaker. Previous studies [33] in ERC have indirectly supported this perspective by observing that some utterances' emotions can be accurately identified without context, while others rely on rich contextual information. Treating both types of utterances uniformly, without considering their underlying causal dynamics, can lead to model degradation.

To explicitly model such causal relationships, we propose a novel Dynamic Causal Prompting Framework (DCPF), which dynamically tailors prompts based on distinct causal types to enhance LLM context modelling. Especially, we classify causal relationships into two types: C1 and C2. In C1, emotion results from accumulated context, reflecting the slow thinking process, while in C2, it emerges rapidly from intense moments and drives the conversation forward, representing the fast thinking process. To distinguish these, we leverage the Peak-End Rule [6], which suggests that people judge experiences based on the most intense ("peak") and final ("end") moments rather than the average. If a target utterance's emotional intensity aligns more with the average intensity of prior utterances, it indicates slow thinking (C1). Conversely, if it aligns with the average of the peak and end intensities, it reflects fast thinking (C2).

To measure the emotional intensity of each utterance, unlike previous methods [30], we consider differences across emotion categories by replacing scalar intensities with full prediction vectors, enabling the model to better capture subtle emotional fluctuations and shifts throughout the conversation. Additionally, we perform causal prompting in each iteration based on updated causal relationships. This dynamic strategy establishes a positive feedback loop between emotion recognition and causal classification. In contrast, static strategies are constrained by the quality of initial causal relationships. In summary, our contributions are as follows:

- We are the first to incorporate fast and slow thinking into the ERC task.
- We propose the DCPF, which dynamically identifies causal relationships using the peak-end rule and generates causal prompts to guide LLMs in context modelling.
- Experimental results on two popular datasets show that the DCPF-based method outperforms state-of-the-art baselines and is effective in both multimodal and text-only settings.

## 2 Related Work

**ERC:** The emotion generation theory [10] emphasizes the importance of contextual information for identifying emotions. Early studies focused on textual modality and modelled context and speaker information [20,35]. However, these approaches still lack commonsense knowledge, which is important for human-like performance [34]. To tackle this, researchers integrated external knowledge sources such as COMET [2] and ConceptNet [29] into their models [7,14,40]. With the increasing relevance of multi-modality in real-world applications, MultiModal Emotion Recognition in Conversation (MERC) has become a focal point of research [27]. In MERC, the fusion of different modalities is crucial, with various approaches being explored, from aggregation-based methods [11,18] to graph-based fusion approaches [4,22]. In recent years, LLMs have achieved remarkable success across a wide range of domains. Therefore, some researchers have applied them to ERC and achieved promising performance [17]. However, LLMs still face challenges in modelling long-range contexts.

**Cause-Effect Discovery:** Traditional methods for causal discovery, such as constraint-based and score-based approaches, have limited direct applicability in NLP due to the unstructured and high-dimensional nature of language data. Instead, researchers have increasingly adopted representation learning and neural methods to uncover latent causal structures from text. Causal reasoning has progressed from early rule-based methods [8,21] to approaches leveraging pre-trained language models for capturing implicit and contextual causality [24,25]. Neural causal discovery methods like CGNN [9] and NOTEARS [41] have inspired adaptations that infer causal structures over discourse elements. Recently, LLMs have shown promising capabilities in encoding causal knowledge [15,36], paving the way for more explainable and reasoning-aware NLP systems. Despite its potential, cause-and-effect reasoning has not yet been explored in ERC tasks.

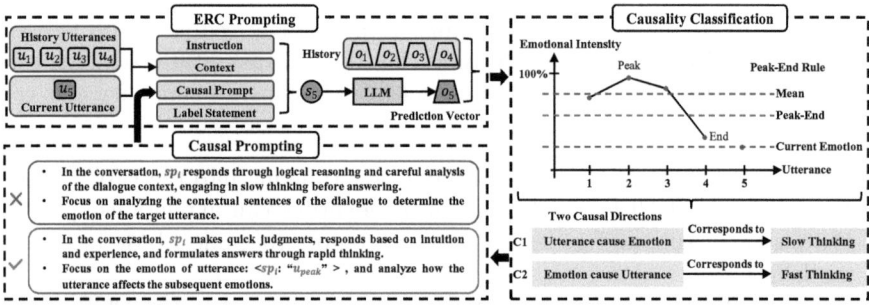

**Fig. 1.** The proposed DCPF framework. Mathematical symbols in the illustration are consistent with the formulas in the paper. The process follows an iterative cycle of ERC Prompting, Causality Classification, and Causal Prompting. In the $t$-th iteration, the Causal Prompting generated in the $(t-1)$-th iteration is used to guide the LLM.

## 3 Methodology

### 3.1 Task Definition

Let $\mathbf{U} = [\mathbf{u}_1, ..., \mathbf{u_N}]$ be a conversation with $\mathbf{N}$ utterances from $\mathbf{M} \geq 2$ speakers, where each $\mathbf{u}_i$ is spoken by $\mathbf{sp}_i$. ERC aims to predict the emotion label $\hat{\mathbf{y}}_i$ for each utterance. The set of predefined emotions is $\mathbf{Y} = [\mathbf{y}_1, ..., \mathbf{y}_\kappa]$, where $\kappa$ is the number of emotion categories.

### 3.2 Framework Overview

To assist the LLM in more effectively modelling contextual information, we propose DCPF, a novel Dynamic Causal Prompting Framework. As illustrated in Fig. 1, DCPF first constructs ERC-specific prompts that convert conversations into structured sequences. Then, we categorise the causal relationship of a conversation into two types and use the Peak-End Rule to classify them. Finally, we design corresponding prompts for the LLM according to the causal relationships and use them in the next iteration for the LLM to predict emotions more accurately, which helps classify causal relationships as positive feedback.

### 3.3 ERC Prompting

Following [17], to effectively adapt LLMs to the ERC task, we design our prompts with three key components: an instruction, the context, and a label statement.

**Instruction:** The instruction component explicitly defines the role for the model. The instruction prompt $\mathcal{P}_{ins}$ is defined as follows:

> **Now you are an expert in sentiment and emotional analysis. The following is the conversation text, which involves several speakers.**

**Context:** To preserve information from previous and current utterances, we incorporate utterances along with their respective speakers. For the target utterance $\mathbf{u}_i$, its context prompt $\mathcal{P}_{his}$ consists of all preceding and current utterances, which is formatted as follows:

> $\mathbf{sp}_1 : \mathbf{u}_1 + \text{<TAB>} + ... + \mathbf{sp}_i : \mathbf{u}_i$

**Label Statement:** To restrict the model's output to a predefined set of emotions and guide its focus on the current utterance, we construct the label statement $\mathcal{P}_{lab}$ as follows:

> **Please select the emotional label of $< \mathbf{sp}_i : \mathbf{u}_i >$ from $< \mathbf{y}_1, ..., \mathbf{y}_\kappa >$**

By combining the three components mentioned above, we transform an utterance $\mathbf{u}_i$ within a conversation into a sequence format $\mathbf{s}_i$, resulting in the final prompt: $\mathcal{P} = \mathcal{P}_{ins} + \mathcal{P}_{his} + \mathcal{P}_{lab}$. Then, we input $\mathbf{s}_i$ into an LLM-based model $f_\theta$, which generates a prediction vector $\mathbf{o}_i = [\mathbf{o}_{i1}, ..., \mathbf{o}_{i\kappa}]$. Here, $\mathbf{o}_{ij}$ represents the probability that $f_\theta$ predicts the emotional category of utterance $\mathbf{u}_i$ as $\mathbf{y}_j$.

## 3.4 Causality Classification

To provide targeted prompts for the LLM, we first categorise conversational causal relationships and align them with fast and slow thinking. These are then classified using the Peak-End Rule, based on which DCPF generates the corresponding causal prompts. We describe the whole process in Algorithm 1.

---

**Algorithm 1:** Dynamic Causal Prompting Framework
---
**Function** *DCPF*:
  **Input**  : $U = [u_1, ..., u_N]$, LLM-based model $f_\theta$
  **Input**  : $U = [u_1, ..., u_N]$, LLM-based model $f_\theta$
  **Output**: Predicted emotional labels $\widehat{Y} = [\widehat{y}_1, ..., \widehat{y}_N]$
  **Output**: Predicted emotional labels $\widehat{Y} = [\widehat{y}_1, ..., \widehat{y}_N]$
  # Calculate emotional intensities
  **for** $i \leftarrow 1$ **to** N **do**
    # Original prompt prediction
    $o_i \leftarrow f_\theta(\mathcal{P}, u_i)$
    $\mathcal{I}_i \leftarrow \|o_i\|_2$
  **for** $i \leftarrow 1$ **to** N **do**
    $\mathcal{C}_{Mean} \leftarrow mean(o_1, ..., o_{i-1})$
    # Select the peak utterance
    $o_{Peak} \leftarrow \arg\max_{j \in \{1,...,i-1\}} (\|o_j\|_2)$
    $o_{End} \leftarrow o_{i-1}$
    $\lambda_{slow} \leftarrow \|\mathcal{I}_i - \mathcal{C}_{Mean}\|_2$
    $\lambda_{fast} \leftarrow \|\mathcal{I}_i - \frac{1}{2}(o_{Peak} + o_{End})\|_2$
    **if** $\lambda_{slow} < \lambda_{fast}$ **then**
      $\mathcal{P}_{cau} \leftarrow \mathcal{P}_{slow}$
    **else**
      $\mathcal{P}_{cau} \leftarrow \mathcal{P}_{fast}$
    $\mathcal{P}' \leftarrow \mathcal{P}_{ins} + \mathcal{P}_{his} + \mathcal{P}_{cau} + \mathcal{P}_{lab}$
    $o'_i \leftarrow f_\theta(\mathcal{P}', u_i)$  // Final prediction
    # Select highest-probability category as result
    $\widehat{y}_i \leftarrow \arg\max_j(o'_i)$
  **return** $\mathcal{Y}$

---

**Causality Categorising:** We categorise the causal relationship in a conversation into two distinct types according to previous work. On one hand, language can be the cause of emotion, where emotion serves as the effect; we name this C1. In C1, emotion results from accumulated context, reflecting the **slow thinking process**. On the other hand, emotion can affect the use of language, where emotion serves as the cause; we call this C2. In C2, emotion emerges rapidly from intense moments and drives the conversation forward, representing the **fast thinking process**.

**Vectorized Intensity:** To track emotional fluctuations in the conversation, we capture the emotional intensity of each utterance. We define the emotional intensity $\mathcal{I}_i$ as the L2 norm of $o_i$, capturing the strength and distribution of emotional signals in the utterance. By computing the intensity arc $\mathcal{I}_1, \mathcal{I}_2, \ldots, \mathcal{I}_N$ across the conversation, we model the affective trajectory of the speaker. However, using a single scalar to represent emotional intensity may overlook important dynamics, especially in conversations with emotional ambiguity or category transitions. Considering differences among emotional categories, we replace scalar intensities with the full prediction vector $\mathbf{o}_i$. Practically, we revise the computation of peak and change-based features accordingly: instead of selecting the utterance with the highest absolute scalar intensity $|\mathcal{I}_i|$ as the peak, we select the one with the largest vector norm $\|\mathbf{o}_i\|_2$; similarly, to evaluate emotional shifts between utterances, we replace scalar absolute differences $|\mathcal{I}_i - \mathcal{I}_j|$ with the Euclidean distance between vectors $\|\mathbf{o}_i - \mathbf{o}_j\|_2$. This vectorised intensity (VI)-based formulation is specialised in reflecting emotional changes in conversations.

**Peak-End Rule:** The peak-end rule is a psychological heuristic suggesting that people judge an experience largely based on how they felt at its most intense moment (the "peak") and at its end, rather than by the average of every moment of the experience. This rule explains why individuals' memories of events are often shaped disproportionately by emotionally charged moments and final impressions. In the context, this means that certain utterances, especially those with high emotional intensity or those occurring at the end, can have a stronger impact on how the overall conversation is perceived emotionally.

– **Slow Thinking**: In slow thinking, emotional responses are more deliberate, with the speaker carefully considering details and analysing rationally. As a result, $\mathbf{o}_i$ tends to align with $\mathcal{C}_{Mean} = 1/\mathbf{N} \sum_{i=1}^{\mathbf{N}} \mathbf{o}_i$. Therefore, $\lambda_{slow} = \|\mathcal{C}_{Mean} - \mathbf{o}_i\|_2$ indicates the proximity of the current utterance to the slow thinking process. A smaller value of $\lambda_{slow}$ suggests that the emotional content of the current utterance is more closely aligned with the slow thinking process.
– **Fast Thinking**: In fast thinking, emotional responses are quick and intense, with the speaker feeling emotions first and expressing them verbally afterwards. Thus, $\mathbf{o}_i$ is likely influenced by $\mathbf{o}_{peak}$ (maximum emotion intensity) and $\mathbf{o}_{end} = \mathbf{o}_{i-1}$ (the last utterance in history). As a result, $\lambda_{fast} = \|(\mathbf{o}_{Peak} + \mathbf{o}_{End})/2 - \mathbf{o}_i\|_2$ indicates the proximity of the current utterance to the fast thinking process. A smaller $\lambda_{fast}$ suggests that the emotion of the current utterance is more closely aligned with the fast thinking process.

Based on the above, if $\lambda_{slow} < \lambda_{fast}$, it indicates that the current utterance follows a slow-thinking process; otherwise, it aligns with a fast-thinking process.

## 3.5 Causal Prompting

We design a specific prompt for LLM according to the causal relationship. For C1, we supply the LLM with a longer context based on the degree to which the current utterance aligns with the slow-thinking process. For example, if the length of the history context is $l$ in the baseline, DCPF will increase it to $l * \lambda_{fast}/\lambda_{slow}$. Moreover, the causal prompt $\mathcal{P}_{cau}$ will be set to $\mathcal{P}_{slow}$:

> In the conversation, sp$_i$ responds through logical reasoning and careful analysis of the context, engaging in slow thinking before answering.
> Focus on analysing the contextual sentences of the conversation to determine the emotion of the target utterance.

For C2, we guide the LLM to focus on the emotion of the peak utterance, so the causal prompt $\mathcal{P}_{cau}$ will be set to $\mathcal{P}_{fast}$:

> In the conversation, sp$_i$ makes quick judgments, responds based on intuition and experience, and formulates answers through rapid thinking.
> Focus on the emotion of utterance: $< sp_i: u_{peak} >$, and analyse how the utterance affects the subsequent emotions.

During each iteration, the LLM-based model $f_\theta$ processes the causal prompting $\mathcal{P}' = \mathcal{P}_{ins} + \mathcal{P}_{his} + \mathcal{P}_{cau} + \mathcal{P}_{lab}$. Then $\mathcal{P}'$ is used to convert conversations to sequences, which serve as input to the LLM.

**Dynamic Prompting:** Based on the emotion predictions from the previous epoch, the model determines the causal relationship and subsequently adjusts the corresponding causal prompts. This updated prompt is then used as input for the next training epoch, allowing the model to adapt its reasoning strategy dynamically. Following each iteration, the model updates its parameters, evolving into $f_{\theta'}$, which serves as the new baseline for subsequent training. In this Dynamic Prompting (DP) framework, on one hand, causal prompts enhance the model's ability for contextual modelling and emotional reasoning; on the other hand, the improved accuracy of emotion prediction conversely enables more reliable classification of causal relationships based on the Peak-End Rule.

## 4 Experiments

### 4.1 Datasets

We conduct experiments on the IEMOCAP [3] and MELD [23] datasets. The statistics are presented in Table 1.

**IEMOCAP** consists of dyadic sessions where actors perform scripted scenarios. And each utterance is labelled with one of the emotions: happy, angry, neutral, sad, excited, or frustrated.

**MELD** is a multi-party conversation dataset collected from the TV show *Friends*, which is an extension of the EmotionLines dataset [5]. Each utterance is annotated with one of the emotions: surprise, fear, disgust, anger, sadness, neutral, or joy, and one of the sentiments: neutral, negative, or positive.

### 4.2 Comparison Models

We benchmark our DCPF framework against a diverse set of models:

**Table 1.** Statistics of two conversational datasets.

| Dataset | Dialogues | | | Utterances | | | Classes |
|---|---|---|---|---|---|---|---|
| | train | val | test | train | val | test | |
| MELD | 1039 | 114 | 280 | 9,989 | 1,109 | 2610 | 7 |
| IEMOCAP | 120 | | 31 | 5,810 | | 1,623 | 6 |

**Table 2.** Per-class F1 scores (%) and W-F1 (%) comparison between our method and different ERC models on IEMOCAP. ★ indicates the source code has been released. ‡ denotes our re-implementation results. ♯, ♭, and ♮ represent results from [12,28], and original papers, respectively.

| Patterns | Methods | IEMOCAP | | | | | | |
|---|---|---|---|---|---|---|---|---|
| | | Happy | Sad | Neutral | Angry | Excited | Frustrated | W-F1 |
| AVT | ★DialogueRNN[♭] | 32.20 | 80.26 | 57.89 | 62.82 | 73.87 | 59.76 | 62.89 |
| AVT | ★MMDFN[♯] | 42.22 | 78.98 | 66.42 | 69.77 | 75.56 | 66.33 | 68.18 |
| AVT | ★M³Net[♭] | 52.74 | 79.39 | 67.55 | 69.30 | 74.39 | 66.58 | 69.24 |
| AVT | MultiEMO[♮] | 52.46 | 83.44 | 71.46 | 66.26 | 73.86 | 67.77 | 70.61 |
| AVT | CMCF-SRNet[♮] | 52.20 | 80.90 | 68.80 | **70.30** | 76.70 | 61.60 | 69.60 |
| AVT | CORECT[♮] | 59.30 | 80.53 | 66.94 | 69.59 | 72.69 | 68.50 | 70.02 |
| AVT | ★SDT[‡] | 56.21 | 75.66 | 68.64 | 65.62 | **80.28** | 63.36 | 69.19 |
| AVT | ★ECERC[♮] | **60.86** | 79.28 | 71.95 | 66.27 | 78.29 | 68.25 | 71.78 |
| VT | ChatGPT[‡] | 52.08 | 64.48 | 54.19 | 37.67 | 39.47 | 52.70 | 50.76 |
| T | ★InstructERC[‡] | - | - | - | - | - | - | 71.39 |
| AVT | EmoLLaMA (Baseline)[‡] | 58.90 | 81.18 | 69.22 | 66.28 | 64.16 | 70.01 | 69.06 |
| AVT | DCPF (Ours) | 58.25 | **84.78** | **72.33** | 68.03 | 72.24 | **70.18** | **71.99** |

**Smaller Models:** We include diverse types of MERC models, including recurrent-based networks (DialogueRNN [20]), transformer-based networks (MultiEmo [27], CMCF-SRNet [39], SDT [19], ECERC [38]), and graph-based networks (M³Net [4], CORECT [22], MMDFN [12]).

**LLM-based Models:** InstructERC [17] reformulates the ERC task from a discriminative framework to a generative framework. Moreover, we prompt ChatGPT on the MERC task and select pictures from videos as visual input.

### 4.3 Experimenal Settings

Because no existing Multimodal LLM (MLLM) has yet been applied to the MERC task, we modify EmoLLaMA [37] and apply it to MERC as the baseline. Consequently, we apply a causal prompt on it to construct DCPF. We conduct a hyperparameter search for our proposed DCPF on each dataset by hold-out validation with a validation set. The hyperparameters to search include learning rate, batch size, and epoch. Given the efficiency and effectiveness of Parameter-

Efficient Fine-Tuning, we adopt LoRA [13] and insert low-rank adapters after the self-attention layers. The adapter dimension is set to 16. All reported results are averages from 5 random test set runs.

**Evaluation Metric:** Following [4], we adopt the weighted F1 score (W-F1) as the primary evaluation metric. For details, we also report per-class F1 scores.

**Table 3.** Per-class F1 scores (%) and W-F1 (%) comparison between our method and different ERC models on MELD.

| Patterns | Methods | MELD | | | | | | |
|---|---|---|---|---|---|---|---|---|
| | | Neutral | Surprise | Fear | Sadness | Joy | Disgust | Anger | W-F1 |
| AVT | ★DialogueRNN$^b$ | 76.97 | 47.69 | - | 20.41 | 50.92 | - | 45.52 | 57.66 |
| AVT | ★MMDFN$^‡$ | 77.76 | 50.69 | - | 22.93 | 54.78 | - | 47.82 | 59.46 |
| AVT | ★M$^3$Net$^b$ | 79.31 | 58.76 | 20.51 | 40.46 | 63.21 | 26.17 | 52.53 | 65.47 |
| AVT | MultiEMO$^b$ | 79.05 | 56.75 | 20.78 | 41.07 | 64.72 | 29.36 | 53.48 | 65.63 |
| AVT | ★SDT$^‡$ | 79.65 | 58.10 | 7.55 | 42.58 | 63.65 | 14.46 | 51.74 | 65.14 |
| AVT | ★ECERC$^b$ | 79.80 | 58.98 | 26.12 | 40.95 | 64.95 | 31.43 | 53.89 | 66.46 |
| VT | ChatGPT$^‡$ | 73.88 | 50.61 | 33.33 | 41.42 | 54.20 | 38.41 | 53.76 | 61.39 |
| T | ★InstructERC$^‡$ | - | - | - | - | - | - | - | 68.24 |
| AVT | EmoLLaMA (Baseline)$^‡$ | **80.33** | **60.27** | 22.22 | 35.42 | 63.78 | **49.12** | 51.73 | 66.34 |
| AVT | DCPF (Ours) | 80.00 | 59.11 | **33.66** | **46.29** | **66.67** | 43.06 | **58.97** | **68.38** |

### 4.4 Overall Results

Tables 2 and 3 compare our DCPF with other methods. Early aggregation-based fusion methods, such as DialogueGCN and SCMM, often overlook the complex interactions between modalities, resulting in suboptimal utilisation of contextual cues. Therefore, most current MERC methods, such as M$^3$Net and MultiEMO, employ graph-based fusion methods to capture interactions between modalities, achieving enhanced performance. More recently, LLMs have gained attention in ERC for their strong contextual reasoning abilities, with even zero-shot ChatGPT surpassing some early aggregation-based models.

Nonetheless, these methods typically lack consideration for the underlying causal dynamics between emotion and context. Our DCPF dynamically determines the model's focus by leveraging the causal relationship between emotion and context, allowing it to selectively attend to the most informative content. This approach achieves state-of-the-art performance in W-F1 scores compared to previous methods, setting a new benchmark in the field. The removal of DCPF causes a decrease of 2.93% in the F1 score for the IEMOCAP dataset and 2.04% for the MELD dataset. This difference in performance improvement may be attributed to the fact that conversations in the IEMOCAP dataset are generally longer and contain more information compared to those in MELD. Moreover, our proposed DCPF achieves state-of-the-art performance in W-F1 scores compared to previous methods, setting a new benchmark in the field, which proves the effectiveness of this framework.

## 4.5 Ablation Study

To investigate the impact of each component of our DCPF, we conducted an ablation study, with results presented in Tables 4 and 5. **w/o** represents the removal operation. The results suggest that all components of the DCPF framework have worked and all the improvements are statistically significant, as evidenced by the paired t-test results with a p-value < 0.05.

Table 4. Ablation study on IEMOCAP dataset.

| Methods | Happy | Sad | Neutral | Angry | Excited | Frustrated | W-F1 |
|---|---|---|---|---|---|---|---|
| Ours | 58.25 | 84.78 | 72.33 | 68.03 | 72.24 | 70.18 | **71.99** |
| w/o VI | 56.33 | 82.80 | 71.65 | 66.32 | 70.33 | 69.66 | 70.70 |
| w/o DP | 63.47 | 82.94 | 69.42 | 67.97 | 66.67 | 69.48 | 70.29 |

Table 5. Ablation study on MELD dataset.

| Methods | Neutral | Surprise | Fear | Sadness | Joy | Disgust | Anger | W-F1 |
|---|---|---|---|---|---|---|---|---|
| Ours | 80.00 | 59.11 | 33.66 | 46.29 | 66.67 | 43.06 | 58.97 | **68.38** |
| w/o VI | 80.04 | 62.21 | 14.93 | 46.80 | 64.01 | 38.38 | 56.06 | 67.50 |
| w/o DP | 79.78 | 61.41 | 30.63 | 43.43 | 64.85 | 42.02 | 54.60 | 67.35 |

Table 6. Comparison of W-F1 performance (%) about Emotional Shift (ES) on the IEMOCAP dataset.

| Methods | ES | non-ES | Total |
|---|---|---|---|
| Ours | 64.22 | 77.61 | 71.99 |
| w/o VI | 60.43 | 77.28 | 70.70 |

**Analysis of Vectorised Intensity:** To track emotional fluctuations in the conversation, we use the probability vector to replace confidence to measure the emotional intensity of each utterance. To prove that VI is sensitive to emotional transitions in conversations, we compare the performance of DCPF and DCPF

**Table 7.** W-F1 performance (%) of baseline and ours across different modalities. A, V, and T represent the acoustic, visual, and textual modalities, respectively.

| Patterns | IEMOCAP | | MELD | |
|---|---|---|---|---|
| | Baseline | Ours | Baseline | Ours |
| T | 66.54 | 69.28 | 64.54 | 66.56 |
| AT | 68.42 | 71.14 | 65.47 | 67.44 |
| VT | 67.28 | 70.39 | 66.00 | 68.20 |
| AVT | 69.06 | 71.99 | 66.34 | 68.38 |

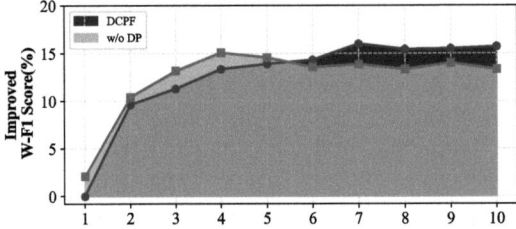

**Fig. 2.** Lifting performance on the first 10 epochs of DCPF and w/o DP compared to the first epoch of DCPF on the validation dataset of IEMOCAP.

**Table 8.** Comparison of Accuracy and W-F1 between DCPF and InstructERC.

| Methods | IEMOCAP | | MELD | |
|---|---|---|---|---|
| | Acc | w-F1 | Acc | w-F1 |
| InstructERC (Baseline) | 67.53 | 67.54 | 67.74 | 66.86 |
| **w/ DCPF** | **70.67** | **70.37** | **69.00** | **68.17** |

w/o VI on emotion shift cases, where consecutive utterances express different emotions. As shown in Table 6, the performance of cases with ES is 13.39% lower than that without ES in DCPF, while the gap increases to 16.85% after the removal of VI. VI significantly improves the performance on ES by 3.79%, and also slightly boosts the performance on nES by 0.33%. This highlights that VI is effective in modelling emotional transitions.

**Analysis of Dynamic Prompting:** To enhance the model's self-improvement ability, we introduce the DP module into DCPF. Figure 2 displays the improved performance over the first 10 epochs. For the model w/o DP, although its improved performance grows rapidly in the early stages, it peaks at 15.05% in epoch 4 and then begins to degrade. In contrast, the w/ DP variant continuously improves through self-iteration, reaching a higher peak of 15.98% at epoch 9, and its performance remains superior in the subsequent epochs. This demonstrates that DP enhances the model's capability for self-optimisation.

## 4.6 Comparison of Different Patterns

Table 7 presents the results of our method across different modality settings. Since DCPF relies on textual prompts to convey causal relationships to the LLM, we only conduct modality comparisons including the textual modality. All DCPF-based models exhibit enhanced performance, emphasising the robust effectiveness of DCPF across diverse modalities. Specifically, DCPF achieves the most significant improvement on the VT modality, with 3.11% on the IEMOCAP dataset and 3.20% on MELD. This suggests that causal prompting can partially mitigate the performance drop caused by the absence of the acoustic modality.

## 4.7 Generalizability Analysis

To verify the robustness of DCPF, we implement our DCPF using InstructERC as the baseline on the text-only ERC task. As shown in Table 8, our proposed DCPF significantly outperforms the baseline, demonstrating its effectiveness and generalisation ability in text-only settings.

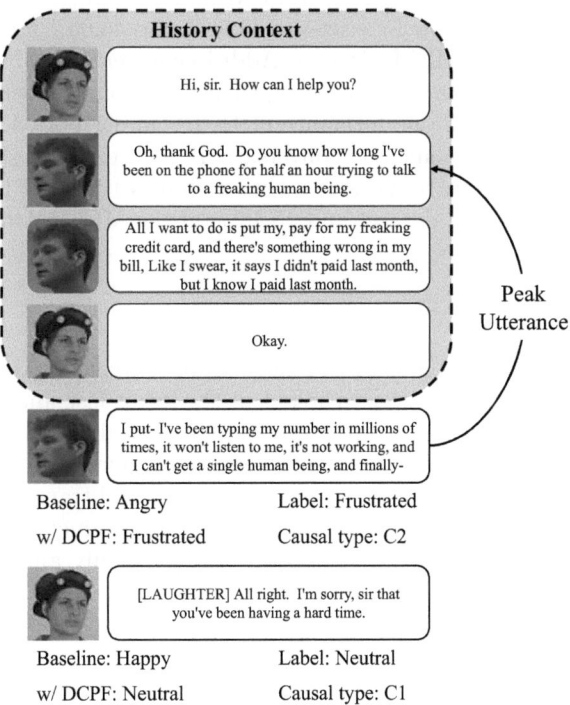

**Fig. 3.** Examples of conversation in the IEMOCAP dataset for the case study. The golden labels for the utterances are highlighted in green font. (Color figure online)

## 4.8 Case Study

As shown in Fig. 3, we select a dialogue between a male and a female speaker as a case study to demonstrate DCPF's improvement in emotion recognition. For the second-to-last utterance, a surface-level interpretation might lead to the mistaken assumption that the male is angry due to an unsuccessful service request. However, within the DCPF framework, male is identified as exhibiting a fast-thinking pattern, where the current utterance is emotionally driven. By referencing cues from the peak utterance, DCPF effectively infers that the male's emotion is not anger toward the service itself, but rather disgust toward the intelligent customer service system. Moreover, for the final utterance, the baseline model incorrectly classifies the emotion as happy simply due to the presence of "[laughter]." In contrast, DCPF recognises that the agent, exhibiting a slow-thinking pattern, is likely expressing polite or formal laughter, and thus correctly categorises the overall emotion as neutral.

## 4.9 Error Analysis

Many prediction errors of our DCPF framework are related to class imbalance, which is evidenced by the low F1 scores of 33.66% and 43.06% for the 'Fear' and 'Disgust' emotions in the MELD dataset. Additionally, emotional shift remains a persistent challenge despite the mitigating effect of VI on this issue. To validate this claim, we analysed the performance of DCPF under both ES and non-ES scenarios. DCPF's performance on conversations with emotion shift samples is consistently lower than those without emotion shift, with a WF1 score drop of 13.39% on the IEMOCAP dataset and 15.43% on the MELD dataset.

# 5 Conclusion

In this paper, we propose the DCPF, a novel dynamic causal prompting framework for ERC. Inspired by the psychological theory of fast and slow thinking, the DCPF adaptively selects prompt strategies based on different causal relationships. By integrating emotion vector representations, our method is more sensitive to emotion shift and can accurately model emotional transitions. Moreover, by conducting causal prompts dynamically, our model conducts self-optimisation during iteration. Extensive experiments on both text-only and MERC benchmarks validate the effectiveness of the DCPF in ERC.

**Acknowledgments.** This work was partially supported by the National Natural Science Foundation of China 62176076, Natural Science Foundation of Guangdong 2023A1515012922, the Shenzhen Foundational Research Funding JCYJ20220818102415032, the Major Key Project of PCL2023A09, and Guangdong Provincial Key Laboratory of Novel Security Intelligence Technologies 2022B1212010005.

# References

1. Barrett, L.F.: Solving the emotion paradox: categorization and the experience of emotion. Pers. Soc. Psychol. Rev. **10**(1), 20–46 (2006)
2. Bosselut, A., Rashkin, H., Sap, M., Malaviya, C., Celikyilmaz, A., Choi, Y.: COMET: commonsense transformers for automatic knowledge graph construction. In: Proceedings of the 57th Annual Meeting of the Association for Computational Linguistics, pp. 4762–4779 (2019)
3. Busso, C., et al.: IEMOCAP: interactive emotional dyadic motion capture database. Lang. Resour. Eval. **42**, 335–359 (2008)
4. Chen, F., Shao, J., Zhu, S., Shen, H.T.: Multivariate, multi-frequency and multimodal: rethinking graph neural networks for emotion recognition in conversation. In: Proceedings of the IEEE/CVF Conference on Computer Vision and Pattern Recognition, pp. 10761–10770 (2023)
5. Chen, S.Y., Hsu, C.C., Kuo, C.C., Ku, L.W., et al.: Emotionlines: an emotion corpus of multi-party conversations. arXiv preprint arXiv:1802.08379 (2018)
6. Epstein, S.: Integration of the cognitive and the psychodynamic unconscious. Am. Psychol. **49**(8), 709 (1994)
7. Ghosal, D., Majumder, N., Gelbukh, A., Mihalcea, R., Poria, S.: Cosmic: commonsense knowledge for emotion identification in conversations. arXiv preprint arXiv:2010.02795 (2020)
8. Girju, R., Badulescu, A., Moldovan, D.: Automatic discovery of part-whole relations. Comput. Linguist. **32**(1), 83–135 (2006)
9. Goudet, O., Kalainathan, D., Caillou, P., Guyon, I., Lopez-Paz, D., Sebag, M.: Learning functional causal models with generative neural networks. In: Explainable and Interpretable Models in Computer Vision and Machine Learning, pp. 39–80 (2018)
10. Gross, J.J., Barrett, L.F.: Emotion generation and emotion regulation: one or two depends on your point of view. Emotion Rev. **3**(1) (2011)
11. Hazarika, D., Poria, S., Mihalcea, R., Cambria, E., Zimmermann, R.: Icon: interactive conversational memory network for multimodal emotion detection. In: Proceedings of the 2018 Conference on Empirical Methods in Natural Language Processing, pp. 2594–2604 (2018)
12. Hu, D., Hou, X., Wei, L., Jiang, L., Mo, Y.: MM-DFN: multimodal dynamic fusion network for emotion recognition in conversations. In: ICASSP 2022-2022 IEEE International Conference on Acoustics, Speech and Signal Processing (ICASSP), pp. 7037–7041. IEEE (2022)
13. Hu, E.J., et al.: Lora: low-rank adaptation of large language models. arXiv preprint arXiv:2106.09685 (2021)
14. Jiang, D., Wei, R., Wen, J., Tu, G., Cambria, E.: AutoML-Emo: automatic knowledge selection using congruent effect for emotion identification in conversations. IEEE Trans. Affect. Comput. **14**(3) (2022)
15. Jin, Z., et al.: CLadder: assessing causal reasoning in language models. Adv. Neural. Inf. Process. Syst. **36**, 31038–31065 (2023)
16. Kahneman, D.: Thinking, fast and slow. macmillan (2011)
17. Lei, S., Dong, G., Wang, X., Wang, K., Wang, S.: InstructERC: reforming emotion recognition in conversation with a retrieval multi-task LLMs framework. CoRR **abs/2309.11911** (2023). https://doi.org/10.48550/ARXIV.2309.11911
18. Lian, Z., Liu, B., Tao, J.: CTNet: conversational transformer network for emotion recognition. IEEE/ACM Trans. Audio, Speech, Lang. Process. **29**, 985–1000 (2021)

19. Ma, H., Wang, J., Lin, H., Zhang, B., Zhang, Y., Xu, B.: A transformer-based model with self-distillation for multimodal emotion recognition in conversations. IEEE Trans. Multimedia **26** (2023)
20. Majumder, N., Poria, S., Hazarika, D., Mihalcea, R., Gelbukh, A., Cambria, E.: DialogueRNN: an attentive RNN for emotion detection in conversations. In: Proceedings of the AAAI Conference on Artificial Intelligence. vol. 33, pp. 6818–6825 (2019)
21. Mirza, P., Tonelli, S.: An analysis of causality between events and its relation to temporal information. In: Proceedings of COLING 2014, the 25th International Conference on Computational Linguistics: Technical Papers, pp. 2097–2106 (2014)
22. Nguyen, C.V.T., Mai, A.T., Le, T.S., Kieu, H.D., Le, D.T.: Conversation understanding using relational temporal graph neural networks with auxiliary cross-modality interaction. arXiv preprint arXiv:2311.04507 (2023)
23. Poria, S., Hazarika, D., Majumder, N., Naik, G., Cambria, E., Mihalcea, R.: Meld: a multimodal multi-party dataset for emotion recognition in conversations. arXiv preprint arXiv:1810.02508 (2018)
24. Rashkin, H., Sap, M., Allaway, E., Smith, N.A., Choi, Y.: Event2Mind: commonsense inference on events, intents, and reactions. arXiv preprint arXiv:1805.06939 (2018)
25. Sap, M., et al.: Atomic: an atlas of machine commonsense for if-then reasoning. In: Proceedings of the AAAI Conference on Artificial Intelligence, vol. 33, pp. 3027–3035 (2019)
26. Satpute, A.B., Shu, J., Weber, J., Roy, M., Ochsner, K.N.: The functional neural architecture of self-reports of affective experience. Biol. Psychiat. **73**(7), 631–638 (2013)
27. Shi, T., Huang, S.L.: Multiemo: an attention-based correlation-aware multimodal fusion framework for emotion recognition in conversations. In: Proceedings of ACL, pp. 14752–14766 (2023)
28. Shi, T., Liang, X., Liang, Y., Tong, X., Huang, S.L.: SSLCL: an efficient model-agnostic supervised contrastive learning framework for emotion recognition in conversations. arXiv preprint arXiv:2310.16676 (2023)
29. Speer, R., Chin, J., Havasi, C.: ConceptNet 5.5: an open multilingual graph of general knowledge. In: Proceedings of the 31st AAAI Conference on Artificial Intelligence, pp. 4444–4451 (2017)
30. Troiano, E., Padó, S., Klinger, R.: Emotion ratings: how intensity, annotation confidence and agreements are entangled. arXiv preprint arXiv:2103.01667 (2021)
31. Tu, G., Jing, R., Liang, B., Yu, Y., Yang, M., Qin, B., Xu, R.: Generalizing to unseen speakers: multimodal emotion recognition in conversations with speaker generalization. IEEE Trans. Affect. Comput. (2025)
32. Tu, G., Liang, B., Jiang, D., Xu, R.: Sentiment-emotion-and context-guided knowledge selection framework for emotion recognition in conversations. IEEE Trans. Affect. Comput. **14**(3), 1803–1816 (2022)
33. Tu, G., Liang, B., Mao, R., Yang, M., Xu, R.: Context or knowledge is not always necessary: a contrastive learning framework for emotion recognition in conversations. In: Findings of the Association for Computational Linguistics: ACL 2023, pp. 14054–14067 (2023)
34. Tu, G., et al.: Multiple knowledge-enhanced interactive graph network for multimodal conversational emotion recognition. In: Findings of the Association for Computational Linguistics: EMNLP 2024, pp. 3861–3874 (2024)

35. Tu, G., Xie, T., Liang, B., Wang, H., Xu, R.: Adaptive graph learning for multi-modal conversational emotion detection. In: Proceedings of the AAAI Conference on Artificial Intelligence, vol. 38, pp. 19089–19097 (2024)
36. Wu, A., et al.: Causality for large language models. arXiv preprint arXiv:2410.15319 (2024)
37. Xing, B., et al.: Emo-Llama: enhancing facial emotion understanding with instruction tuning. arXiv preprint arXiv:2408.11424 (2024)
38. Zhang, T., Tan, Z.: ECERC: evidence-cause attention network for multi-modal emotion recognition in conversation. In: Proceedings of the 63rd Annual Meeting of the Association for Computational Linguistics (Volume 1: Long Papers), pp. 2064–2077 (2025)
39. Zhang, X., Li, Y.: A cross-modality context fusion and semantic refinement network for emotion recognition in conversation. In: Proceedings of the 61st Annual Meeting of the Association for Computational Linguistics (Volume 1: Long Papers), pp. 13099–13110 (2023)
40. Zhao, W., Zhao, Y., Lu, X.: CauAIN: causal aware interaction network for emotion recognition in conversations. In: IJCAI, pp. 4524–4530 (2022)
41. Zheng, X., Aragam, B., Ravikumar, P.K., Xing, E.P.: DAGs with NO TEARS: continuous optimization for structure learning. Adv. Neural Info. Process. Syst. **31** (2018)

# 3D Path Planning for UAVs in Complex Environments Using an Improved Hybrid Genetic-PSO Algorithm

Xiuqin Pan[✉], Shuyun Zhang, and Xuze Gu

Minzu University of China, No. 27 Zhongguancun South Street, Haidian District, Beijing, China

amycun@163.com

**Abstract.** This paper proposes an Improved Hybrid Genetic Particle Swarm Algorithm (IHGPA) to address the limitations of conventional methods in UAV 3D path planning for mountainous environments. IHGPA effectively combines the mechanisms of Particle Swarm Optimization (PSO) and Genetic Algorithm (GA) into a single hybrid architecture. This system employs adaptive parameter control and integrates genetic operation strategies to maintain population diversity and mitigate early convergence. Furthermore, it utilizes a Gaussian-represented terrain modeling approach and a multi-criteria fitness function to simultaneously optimize path safety, trajectory smoothness, and routing efficiency. Experimental results demonstrate that IHGPA achieves superior convergence speed and solution quality, reducing final cost by 6.0% and 2.1% compared to standard PSO and GA, respectively. This work provides an effective reference for autonomous UAV navigation in complex terrains.

**Keywords:** Unmanned Aerial Vehicle (UAV) · Path Planning · 3D Terrain · Particle Swarm Optimization (PSO) · Genetic Algorithm (GA)

## 1 Introduction

Unmanned Aerial Vehicles (UAVs) are playing an increasingly critical role in applications such as aerial mapping, disaster response, and infrastructure inspection. However, path planning in complex mountainous terrain remains a major challenge, where generating smooth, efficient, and safe trajectories is essential for autonomous operation [1]. While conventional algorithms like Dijkstra's perform well in structured environments, they lack adaptability and efficiency in unstructured 3D spaces. Intelligent optimization methods like PSO and GA enable global search but struggle with slow convergence, local optima entrapment, and poor path quality. These limitations highlight the need for a terrain-adaptive, efficient, and reliable path planning method with strong practical applicability, representing significant theoretical and practical value for autonomous UAV operations in complex environments.

Recent research in path planning emphasizes hybrid swarm intelligence algorithms that merge complementary optimization techniques. For example, PSO's fast convergence and GA's global search capability are often combined in hybrid models to improve overall performance. Despite these advances, current hybrid methods still struggle with key challenges including parameter adaptation, satisfaction of multiple constraints—such as obstacle avoidance, path length, and altitude limitations in 3D environments—as well as insufficient robustness. Addressing these limitations remains essential for developing more capable and adaptive path planning algorithms [3].

To address these challenges, this paper proposes an Improved Hybrid Genetic Particle Swarm Algorithm (IHGPA) for efficient and safe UAV path planning in complex 3D terrains. Key contributions include: a 3D dynamic terrain model using superimposed Gaussian functions to simulate mountainous environments; a hybrid optimization mechanism combining adaptive parameter adjustment and genetic operations to improve convergence and stability; a multi-objective fitness function incorporating collision [2], length, and smoothness penalties to enhance path quality; and comparative experiments validating the algorithm's superiority in convergence speed, path quality, and robustness.

## 2 Related Theoretical Foundations

### 2.1 UAV Path Planning Problem Modeling

#### 2.1.1 Environmental Model

The environment is represented as a discrete grid $T(x, y) \in R^{M \times N}$, where M and N denote the grid dimensions, and $T(x, y)$ returns the terrain elevation at coordinate (x, y). The terrain is constructed using superimposed Gaussian functions with smoothing to simulate realistic mountainous regions, including randomized peaks and natural variations [4]. A path $P = [p_0, p_1, \ldots, p_L]$ consists of a sequence of 3D waypoints from start $S = (x_s, y_s, z_s)$ to goal $E = (x_e, y_e, z_e)$, where each $P = [p_0, p_1, \ldots, p_L]$ denotes a waypoint.

#### 2.1.2 Constraints

**Safety Constraint:** All path points and intermediate sampled points along segments must maintain a minimum safe altitude [5]: $z_i \geq T(x_i, y_i) + h_{\text{safe}}$, where $h_{\text{safe}}$ is the basic safety margin.

**Smoothness Constraint:** The turning angle between any three consecutive waypoints must not exceed the UAV's maximum turning angle $\theta_{\max}=60°$, i.e., $(p_{i-2}p_{i-1}p_i) \leq \theta_{\max}$, ensuring feasible maneuverability [7].

**Height Constraint:** Path altitude must remain within a reasonable operational range $T(x_i, y_i) + h_{\text{safe}} + h_{\text{buffer}} \leq z_i \leq H_{\max} \cdot r_{\text{safe}}$.

**Boundary Constraint:** All waypoints must lie within the defined map boundaries.

### 2.2 Particle Swarm Optimization (PSO)

Particle Swarm Optimization (PSO) is a stochastic optimization technique inspired by the collective foraging behavior of bird flocks [8]. In PSO, each candidate solution is represented as a "particle" that navigates the solution space by updating its velocity and position iteratively [9, 10]. The movement of each particle is influenced by its own best-known position (pbest$_t$) and the best-known position across the entire swarm (gbest) [21]. This mechanism facilitates efficient global optimization and is particularly valued in path planning applications due to its rapid convergence and straightforward implementation. The velocity and position of each particle are updated according to the following equations [6]:

$$v_i^t = w \cdot v_i^{t-1} + c_1 \cdot r_1 \cdot \left(pbest_i - x_i^{t-1}\right) + c_2 \cdot r_2 \cdot \left(gbest - x_i^{t-1}\right) \tag{1}$$

$$x_i^t = x_i^{t-1} + v_i^t \tag{2}$$

In the algorithm, $v_i^t$ and $x_i^t$ denote the velocity and position of particle $i$ at iteration $t$ [8], where $w$ is the inertia weight controlling velocity retention.;$c_1$ and $c_2$ are acceleration coefficients;while *pbest$_i$* and *gbest* represent the particle's and swarm's historical best positions, respectively [9]. However, conventional PSO suffers from limitations such as high parameter sensitivity, poor high-dimensional performance, and limited diversity [5].

### 2.3 Genetic Algorithm

The Genetic Algorithm (GA) is an optimization technique modeled on natural evolution, which utilizes selection, crossover, and mutation to evolve solutions toward optimality. Known for its strong global search ability and robustness [11], GA is often combined with other algorithms to improve performance. Key operations such as selection, crossover, and mutation iteratively evolve the population. Individuals are chosen probabilistically based on fitness using methods like roulette wheel selection. Selected parents then undergo genetic recombination to produce offspring that inherit favorable traits, as expressed in the following formula [12], Mutation introduces new genetic material by randomly altering genes, thereby helping to maintain population diversity [13].

$$x_{child1} = \alpha \cdot x_{parent1} + (1 - \alpha) \cdot x_{parent2} \tag{3}$$

$$x_{child2} = \alpha \cdot x_{parent2} + (1 - \alpha) \cdot x_{parent1} \tag{4}$$

## 3 Design of the Improved Hybrid Genetic-Particle Algorithm (IHGPA)

### 3.1 Overall Framework of the IHGPA

The Improved Hybrid Genetic Particle Algorithm (IHGPA) combines PSO's fast convergence with GA's crossover and mutation to enhance diversity and avoid local optima [14]. Key steps include:

**Population Initialization:** Particles represent 3D paths with fixed start/end points. Intermediate points are randomly initialized within safe altitude bounds.

**PSO Iterative Optimization:** PSO Iterative Optimization: Particles update velocity and position using individual and global best solutions.

**GA Operations:** Genetic operations—selection, crossover, and mutation—are performed every 10 iterations to enhance population diversity.

**Dynamic Parameter Adjustment**: Parameters including inertia weight, acceleration coefficients, and genetic operation probabilities are dynamically adjusted during iteration to balance exploration and exploitation [15].

**Convergence Criteria:** The algorithm terminates either after 500 iterations or when the global best solution stabilizes with no further improvement.

## 3.2 Dynamic Parameter Adjustment Strategy

### 3.2.1 PSO Parameter Adjustment

**Inertia weight:** A higher initial w enhances global exploration, while a lower w later improves local exploitation [16]. The formula is:

$$w = w_{\max} - (w_{\max} - w_{\min}) \cdot \frac{t}{t_{\max}} \tag{5}$$

where $w_{\max} = 0.9$, $w_{\min} = 0.4$, $t$ is the current iteration count, and $t_{\max} = 500$

**Acceleration factor:** The acceleration coefficients $c_1$, $c_2$ guide particles toward their personal best and the global best, respectively. A higher $c_1$ promotes individual exploration in early stages, while a larger $c_2$ enhances collective convergence later in the process [17]. The calculation formulas are:

$$c_1 = c_{1,\text{ini}} - (c_{1,\text{ini}} - c_{1,\text{fin}}) \cdot \frac{t}{t_{\max}} \tag{6}$$

$$c_2 = c_{2,\text{ini}} - (c_{2,\text{ini}} - c_{2,\text{fin}}) \cdot \frac{t}{t_{\max}} \tag{7}$$

where $c_{1,\text{ini}} = c_{2,\text{ini}} = 2.0$, $c_{1,\text{fin}} = c_{2,\text{fin}} = 0.5$

### 3.2.2 GA Parameter Adjustment

The crossover probability $P_c$ and mutation probability $P_m$ adopt an exponential decay strategy to balance diversity and convergence. Initially set to a high value (e.g., $P_{c,\text{ini}} = 0.9$) to encourage exploration, $P_c$ gradually decreases according to an exponential function [18].

$$P_c = P_{c,\text{ini}} \cdot \exp(-\lambda_1 \cdot t), \left(P_{c,\text{ini}} = 0.9, \lambda_2 = 0.01\right) \tag{8}$$

Mutation Probability $P_m$: Moderately high early ($P_{m,\text{ini}} = 0.1$) to maintain diversity, reduced later to preserve stability:

$$P_m = P_{m,\text{ini}} \cdot \exp(-\lambda_2 \cdot t) \tag{9}$$

## 3.3 Fitness Function Design

The fitness function assesses path quality using a multi-objective formulation that considers safety, efficiency, and smoothness [18]:

$$\text{TotalCost} = w_{\text{col}} \cdot C_{\text{col}} + C_{\text{h}} + w_{\text{len}} \cdot C_{\text{len}} + w_{\text{sm}} \cdot C_{\text{sm}} \tag{10}$$

where $C_{\text{col}}$、$C_{\text{h}}$、$C_{\text{len}}$、$C_{\text{sm}}$ denote collision, height, length, and smoothness costs, and $w_{\text{col}}$、$w_{\text{len}}$、$w_{\text{sm}}$ are adaptive weights [19]. The collision cost $C_{\text{col}}$ implements obstacle avoidance through dual detection: point verification ($z_i \geq T(x_i, y_i) + h_{\text{safe}}$) and segment inspection (10 intermediate points). Total cost sums all violation penalties. The height cost $C_{\text{h}}$ applies bidirectional penalties: for collision risk (too low) and energy efficiency (too high). The length cost $C_{\text{len}}$ promotes efficiency by penalizing total Euclidean distance between path points. The smoothness cost $C_{\text{sm}}$ enforces kinematic constraints by penalizing excessive turning angles. Weight coefficients $w_{\text{col}}$, $w_{\text{len}}$, and $w_{\text{sm}}$ adapt dynamically based on iteration progress and path quality. Their adjustment strategies are defined as follows [20]:

$$w_{\text{col}} = w_{\text{col,base}} \cdot (1 + \min(1.0, \text{collision\_count}/L)) \tag{11}$$

$$w_{\text{sm}} = w_{\text{sm,base}} \cdot (1 + 0.5 \cdot t/t_{\text{max}}) \tag{12}$$

$$w_{\text{len}} = w_{\text{len,base}} \cdot (1 + 0.5 \cdot t/t_{\text{max}}) \tag{13}$$

## 3.4 Path Generation and Constraint Handling

The start $S = (10,10,20)$ and end $E = (90,90,80)$ of the path remain fixed to define the mission scope. Intermediate points $p_i (1 \leq i \leq L - 2)$ are initialized randomly, with their height restricted to $\left[T(x_i, y_i) + h_{\text{safe}} + h_{\text{buffer}}, H_{\text{max}} \cdot r_{\text{safe}}\right]$ to prevent initial collisions. Path adjustments, governed by particle velocity, are constrained in speed and updated in real time to avoid abrupt changes. Compute the magnitude $|v_i|$ of the velocity vector. If it exceeds the maximum speed $v_{\text{max}} = 5.0$, scale it proportionally: $v_{i'} = v_i \cdot \frac{v_{\text{max}}}{|v_i|}$. Update each waypoint coordinate via $p_i = p_i + v_i$ to maintain smooth motion [18].

## 4 Experimental Analysis

### 4.1 Experimental Setup

Experimental Environment

| hardware | CPU Intel, memory 32GB |
|---|---|
| Software | Python 3.8, Matplotlib 3.5, NumPy 1.21 |

### 4.1.1 3D Terrain Generation Utilizing Superimposed Gaussian Functions and Gaussian Filtering

Smooth mountainous terrain was generated by superimposing multiple Gaussian functions and applying Gaussian filtering:

$$Z(x, y) = \sum_{k=1}^{N} H_k \exp\left(-\frac{(x-x_k)^2}{2\sigma_x^2} - \frac{(y-y_k)^2}{2\sigma_y^2}\right) \tag{14}$$

where N denotes the number of peaks, with a value ranging from 5 to 15 to ensure moderate terrain complexity $(x_k, y_k)$ The peak center coordinates are uniformly distributed at random within a 100 × 100 map area. The distribution parameters $\sigma_x$ and $\sigma_y$ denote the standard deviations of the k-th peak along the x and y directions, respectively, with values ranging from 10 to 30. The peak height $H_k$ follows a uniform distribution between 5 and 30 [19]. Gaussian filtering with a kernel size of σ = smoothness is applied to enhance terrain continuity. To further improve topological coherence and realism, the generated terrain is smoothed using Gaussian filtering [20]:

$$Z_{\text{smooth}} = G_\sigma * Z \tag{15}$$

### 4.1.2 Algorithm Parameter Configuration (Table 1)

Table 1. Parameter Settings Table

| Parameter categories | Parameter name | short-cut process |
|---|---|---|
| Map parameters | Map size | 100100100 |
| | Maximum obstacle height | 30 |
| | smoothness | 5 |
| PSO parameter | population size | 200 |
| | Maximum number of iterations | 1000 |
| | Inertia weight range | [0.4,0.9] |
| | Accelerator factor range | [0.5,2.0] |
| GA parameter | Initial cross probability | 0.9 |
| | Initial mutation probability | 0.1 |
| Path parameters | Number of path points | 20 |
| | safety height | 5 |
| | Maximum turning height | 60° |

## 4.2 Experimental Results and Analysis

### 4.2.1 Algorithm Convergence Analysis

**Overal Convergence Trend:** Convergence speed and stability are key performance indicators. As shown in Fig. 1 (Algorithm Convergence Curves), IHGPA decreases sharply in early iterations, reflecting strong global exploration and rapid convergence to high-quality solutions, while standard PSO and GA converge more slowly.

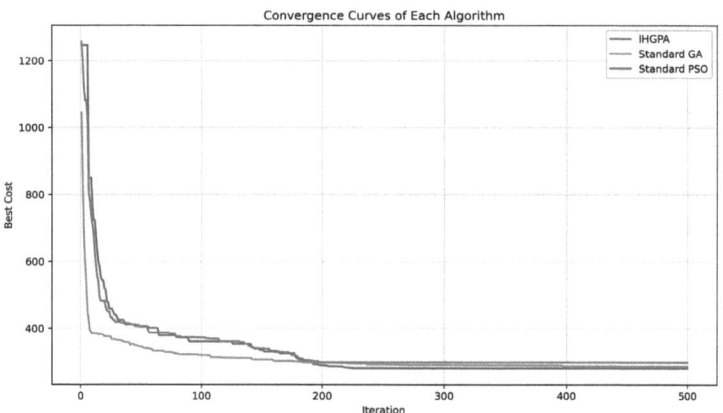

**Fig. 1.** Algorithm Convergence Curves

**Early-Stage Convergence Analysis:** Fig. 2 illustrates the convergence trends of each algorithm during the initial 100 iterations. IHGPA reduced its cost from approximately 1200 to around 400 within the first 100 iterations, demonstrating a significantly faster convergence rate than both PSO and GA. During this phase, standard PSO and GA exhibited noticeable oscillations, reflecting inefficient global search and a tendency to become trapped in local optima. These results confirm that the integration of genetic operations (selection, crossover, and mutation) in IHGPA enhances population diversity, prevents premature convergence, and accelerates early-stage search.

**Stabilization Phase Performance:** As shown in Fig. 3 (Algorithm Convergence Curves – Full Process), IHGPA stabilized after around 200 iterations, converging to an optimal cost of approximately 280. In contrast, both standard PSO and GA exhibited continued fluctuations until the final iterations (~500), with best costs around 298 and 286, respectively, demonstrating lower stability than IHGPA. These results demonstrate that IHGPA's adaptive parameter strategy—featuring a linearly decreasing inertia weight w and tunable learning factors $c_1$ and $c_2$—effectively balances global exploration and local exploitation, along with exponentially decaying crossover and mutation probabilities—effectively balances exploration and exploitation across search phases, enabling faster convergence and more stable solutions.

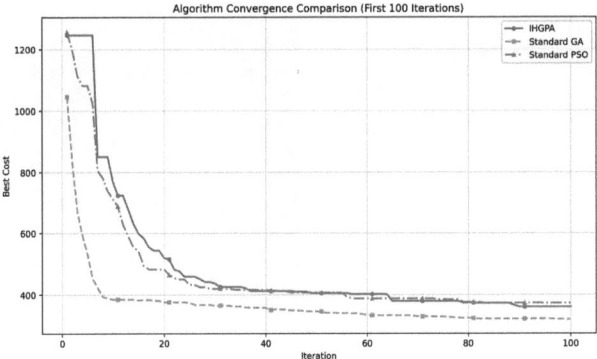

**Fig. 2.** Convergence Performance within Initial 100 Iterations

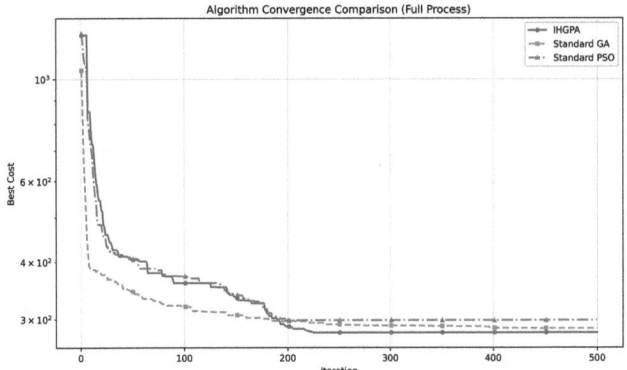

**Fig. 3.** Algorithm Convergence Curves – Full Process

### 4.2.2 Final Performance and Optimization Margin

After 500 iterations, the optimal cost values for IHGPA, GA, and PSO are 280.57, 286.49, and 298.47, respectively. IHGPA achieves the lowest cost, demonstrating its ability to escape local optima and deliver globally superior paths.

The optimization margins—reflecting total cost reduction—are 77.5% for IHGPA, 72.6% for GA, and 76.3% for PSO. This improvement confirms IHGPA's comprehensive advantage in multi-objective optimization, including safety, smoothness, and altitude rationality.

### 4.3 Comprehensive Analysis of Path Planning Quality

The 3D path generated by IHGPA shows excellent performance in complex mountainous terrain. As illustrated, the red path closely follows terrain contours, effectively avoids obstacles, and maintains a safe altitude. Its 2D projection is smooth without unnecessary detours, and all turns occur in flat areas, reflecting strengths in safety, efficiency, and feasibility. IHGPA achieves the lowest total cost, with superior obstacle avoidance, balanced altitude, smooth trajectory, and economical path length (Fig. 4).

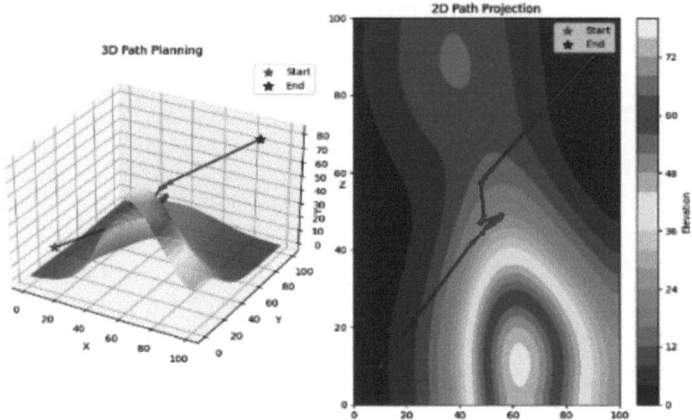

**Fig. 4.** 3D path planning map

## 5 Conclusion

This paper proposes an Improved Hybrid Genetic Particle Swarm Algorithm (IHGPA) for UAV path planning in complex 3D environments. IHGPA combines the rapid convergence of Particle Swarm Optimization with the global exploration capacity of Genetic Algorithms through improvements in algorithmic structure, fitness evaluation, and adaptive parameter mechanisms. The dynamic parameter adaptation and adaptive genetic operations mitigate premature convergence in PSO and slow convergence in GA, balancing solution quality and computational efficiency. Experimental results demonstrate that IHGPA achieves the lowest total cost (280.57) with faster convergence, strong initial search efficiency, stable optimization behavior, and robust performance.

## References

1. Puente-Castro, A., Rivero, D., Pazos, A., Fernandez-Blanco, E.: A review of artificial intelligence applied to path planning in UAV swarms. Neural Comput. Appl. **34**(1), 153–170 (2022)
2. Saeed, R.A., Omri, M., Abdel-Khalek, S., Ali, E.S., Alotaibi, M.F.: Optimal path planning for drones based on swarm intelligence algorithm. Neural Comput. Appl. **34**(12), 10133–10155 (2022)
3. Roberge, V., Tarbouchi, M., Labonté, G.: Comparison of parallel genetic algorithm and particle swarm optimization for real-time UAV path planning. IEEE Trans. Industr. Inf. **9**(1), 132–141 (2012)
4. Sharma, A., Shoval, S., Sharma, A., Pandey, J.K.: Path planning for multiple targets interception by the swarm of UAVs based on swarm intelligence algorithms: a review. IETE Tech. Rev. **39**(3), 675–697 (2022)
5. He, W., Qi, X., Liu, L.: A novel hybrid particle swarm optimization for multi-UAV cooperate path planning. Appl. Intell. **51**(10), 7350–7364 (2021)
6. Shao, S., Peng, Y., He, C., Du, Y.: Efficient path planning for UAV formation via comprehensively improved particle swarm optimization. ISA Trans. **97**, 415–430 (2020)

7. Deng, L., Chen, H., Zhang, X., Liu, H.: Three-dimensional path planning of UAV based on improved particle swarm optimization. Mathematics **11**(9), 1987 (2023)
8. Tang, J., Duan, H., Lao, S.: Swarm intelligence algorithms for multiple unmanned aerial vehicles collaboration: a comprehensive review. Artif. Intell. Rev. **56**(5), 4295–4327 (2023)
9. Foo, J.L., Knutzon, J., Kalivarapu, V., Oliver, J., Winer, E.: Path planning of unmanned aerial vehicles using B-splines and particle swarm optimization. J. Aerosp. Comput. Inf. Commun. **6**(4), 271–290 (2009)
10. Huang, C., Fei, J.: UAV path planning based on particle swarm optimization with global best path competition. Int. J. Pattern Recognit Artif Intell. **32**(06), 1859008 (2018)
11. Liu, Y., Zhang, H., Zheng, H., Li, Q., Tian, Q.: A spherical vector-based adaptive evolutionary particle swarm optimization for UAV path planning under threat conditions. Sci. Rep. **15**(1), 2116 (2025)
12. Meng, Z., Li, D., Zhang, Y., Yan, H.: Intelligent scheduling technology of swarm intelligence algorithm for drone path planning. Drones **8**(4), 120 (2024)
13. Zhao, Y., Zheng, Z., Liu, Y.: Survey on computational-intelligence-based UAV path planning. Knowl.-Based Syst. **158**, 54–64 (2018)
14. Fu, Y., Ding, M., Zhou, C., Hu, H.: Route planning for unmanned aerial vehicle (UAV) on the sea using hybrid differential evolution and quantum-behaved particle swarm optimization. IEEE Transactions on Systems, Man, and Cybernetics: Systems **43**(6), 1451–1465 (2013)
15. Goel, U., Varshney, S., Jain, A., Maheshwari, S., Shukla, A.: Three dimensional path planning for UAVs in dynamic environment using glow-worm swarm optimization. Procedia Computer Science **133**, 230–239 (2018)
16. Ye, Z., Li, H., Wei, W.: Improved particle swarm optimization based on multi-strategy fusion for UAV path planning. International Journal of Intelligent Computing and Cybernetics **17**(2), 213–235 (2024)
17. Huang, C., Zhou, X., Ran, X., Wang, J., Chen, H., Deng, W.: Adaptive cylinder vector particle swarm optimization with differential evolution for UAV path planning. Eng. Appl. Artif. Intell. **121**, 105942 (2023)
18. Shao, Z., Yan, F., Zhou, Z., Zhu, X.: Path planning for multi-UAV formation rendezvous based on distributed cooperative particle swarm optimization. Appl. Sci. **9**(13), 2621 (2019)
19. Rosas-Carrillo, A.S., Solís-Santomé, A., Silva-Sánchez, C., Camacho-Nieto, O.: UAV path planning using an adaptive strategy for the particle swarm optimization algorithm. Drones **9**(3), 170 (2025)
20. Ji, Y., Liu, Q., Zhou, C., Han, Z., Wu, W.: Hybrid swarm intelligence and human-inspired optimization for urban drone path planning. Biomimetics **10**(3), 180 (2025)
21. Phung, M.D., Quach, C.H., Dinh, T.H., Ha, Q.: Enhanced discrete particle swarm optimization path planning for UAV vision-based surface inspection. Autom. Constr. **81**, 25–33 (2017)

# Application and Industry Track

# Research on Algorithms Based on Autoregressive Fusion Models

Xiaoling Wang(✉)

Information Technology Center, National Offshore Oil Corporation (CNOOC) Limited, Beijing, China
wangxl3@cnooc.com.cn

**Abstract.** Operating revenue is a core metric for firm value chain analysis, impacting profit forecasting, resource allocation, and strategy. Traditional methods often leads to high error rates, exceeding 20% in oil-price or operation revenue-related forecasts for cyclical industries like energy. We propose a novel hybrid framework integrating dynamic feature engineering with an enhanced SARIMA model. Our key innovations are: (1) A dynamic pre-processing pipeline significantly improving data stationarity; (2) An intelligent parameter search combining grid search with Bayesian criteria reduces error rates by 18.5%; (3) Empirical results demonstrate superior performance: for energy revenue forecasting, the model achieves a 20-step ahead forecast error standard deviation within ± 5%. Future work will explore integrating LSTM-Transformer modules for nonlinear features, reducing grid search time consumption by enabling intelligent optimization to automatically skip invalid parameter combinations. On the other hand, embedding predictive models into ERP applications will deliver enhanced data value to users.

**Keywords:** SARIMA · ARIMA · ADF · ACF · PACF · RMS · Autoregressive Algorithm · Time Series Analysis

## 1 Introduction

The Value of Corporate Revenue and Accounts Receivable Data, and the Significance of Revenue Forecasting Enterprises seek to maximize value by optimizing their capital structure to balance debt returns and associated risks. Operating revenue, as a core internal factor influencing capital structure, directly correlates with a firm's debt-servicing capacity through its stability. Meanwhile, accounts receivable represent potential risk liabilities, necessitating dynamic monitoring to enhance asset liquidity. Consequently, analyzing operating revenue and accounts receivable data serves as a critical entry point for evaluating corporate financial health.

In comprehensive budget management, enterprises must integrate business operations, information flows, and capital movements, leveraging methods such as rolling forecasts to reconcile discrepancies between actual performance and target objectives. For instance, the accuracy of revenue forecasting directly determines the depth of profit variance analysis, thereby guiding strategic adjustments. Effective revenue forecasting not only optimizes resource allocation but also enhances risk resilience by enabling early identification of market fluctuations.

## 2 Mainstream Revenue Forecasting Methods and Existing Challenges

Current mainstream methods for corporate revenue forecasting can be broadly categorized into the following three groups, though each exhibits certain limitations:

### 2.1 Traditional Statistical Models

(1) Time series analysis (such as moving averages, exponential smoothing): Relies on the periodic patterns of historical data and is suitable for short-term forecasting, but struggles to capture nonlinear relationships and the impacts of external factors (e.g., policy changes, competitive dynamics).
(2) Regression analysis: Sensitive to data stationarity/multi-collinearity and incompatible with high-dimensional temporal features.
(3) Critical gap: Assumes linear decomposability while neglecting dynamic market correlations, causing significant long-term deviations. Hypothesis: SARIMA with dynamic preprocessing outperforms ARIMA in non-stationary seasonal data.

### 2.2 Machine Learning Methods

(1) Ensemble Learning and Tree Models (such as Random Forest, XGBoost): These models excel at handling multi-source heterogeneous data but have relatively weak capabilities in modeling temporal dependencies.
(2) Long Short-Term Memory Networks (LSTM): Leveraging memory cells and gating mechanisms, LSTMs can capture long-term dependencies and have been successfully applied to revenue forecasting in fields like e-commerce and energy. For instance, Guangzhou Hexing Tech Innovation (electricity sales). Limitations: Data-hungry, computationally intensive, and complex hyper-parameter tuning.

#### 2.2.1 Hybrid Models and Emerging Technologies

(1) LSTM + Attention Mechanism: Reduces noise but suffers interpretability issues.
(2) Multivariate LSTM: By integrating external factors (such as economic indicators and competitive data), it overcomes the limitations of single-sequence forecasting. For example, Great Wall Motor (automotive revenue).Critical limitation: Excludes real-time exogenous variables (oil prices, policy shocks) for model simplicity.
(3) Transformer hybrids: Address non-linearity better than pure ML models, posing a relatively high application threshold for small and medium-sized enterprises (SMEs).

#### 2.2.2 Research Advancements and Algorithm Optimization Directions

Recent focus (2024–2025) addresses core challenges:

(1) Dynamic Feature Extraction: Enhancing the model's adaptability to complex patterns by segmenting fluctuations (e.g., separating long-term trends from short-term fluctuations), Industry impact:22% accuracy gain in oil & gas (IEA, 2025);

(2) Error Correction Mechanisms: Introducing rolling forecasts and feedback loops to mitigate the error accumulation problem in multi-step forecasting with LSTMs. Reduces LSTM step-error by 30%;
(3) Computational Efficiency: Innovation is in Bayesian optimization vs. grid search, and cuts search time by 65% for large datasets;

Enhanced Interpretability: Analyzing the LSTM decision-making process with tools such as SHAP values to improve the credibility of forecasting results, Meets financial compliance requirements.

## 3 Overview of Revenue Forecasting Algorithms

The Seasonal ARIMA (SARIMA) model significantly enhances the fitting capability for complex time series by introducing seasonal differencing and periodic parameters. Critically, SARIMA with dynamic preprocessing demonstrates superior forecasting performance over standard ARIMA when handling non-stationary seasonal data. For our limited-sample dataset, we implement a hybrid optimization approach combining grid search with Bayesian-optimized AIC criteria. This methodology selection follows extensive preliminary validation confirming a distinct 12-month cyclical pattern in the data, which directly informs our seasonal parameter specification.

This study takes monthly data as an example (from January 2015 to December 2019) and aims to address the following questions:

(1) How to identify the stationarity and seasonality of a sequence through statistical tests and visualization methods;
(2) How to determine the optimal model parameters using ACF/PACF plots and grid search;
(3) How to evaluate the model's forecasting performance and validate its effectiveness.

Research Objectives:
Understand the fundamental characteristics of the data through time series analysis, stationarity detection, seasonal decomposition, and autocorrelation analysis.
Model Selection and Fitting: Use BIC and AIC as criteria to select the best ARIMA/SARIMA model.
Forecasting and Evaluation: Predict future data and evaluate the model's forecasting performance using RMSE.

### 3.1 Data and Research Methodology

Before determining which algorithm model to select for revenue data forecasting, it is necessary to make a preliminary assessment of the data being analyzed in order to choose an appropriate algorithm model. The data comprises 60 months of observations, exhibiting significant annual cyclical fluctuations and an overall trend that first rises and then declines. Further tests for stationarity are required (the data is sourced from enterprise operational management data and has been desensitized), as illustrated in Fig. 1.

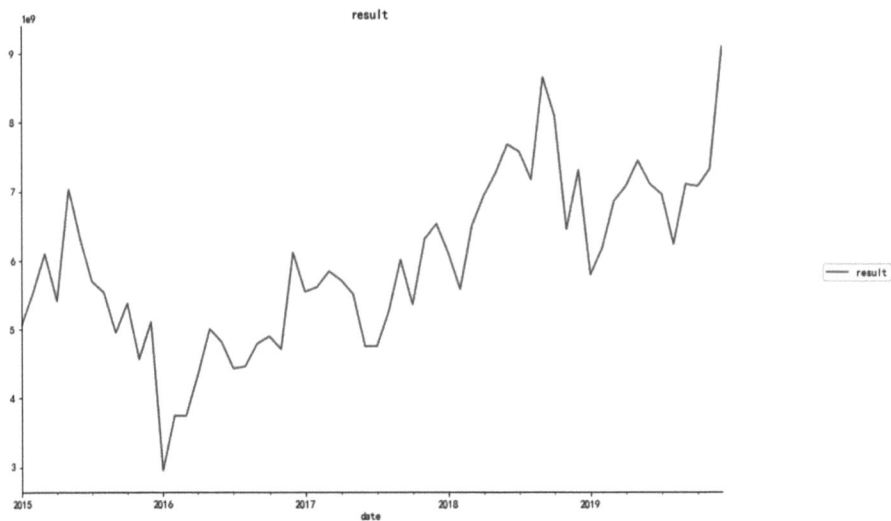

**Fig. 1.** Analysis of Data Trend Changes

### 3.1.1 Stationarity Test and Differencing

Time series modeling requires the data to meet the stationarity condition (constant mean and variance). In this study, the Augmented Dickey-Fuller (ADF) test is employed:

Null Hypothesis ($H_0$): The series is non-stationary.
Alternative Hypothesis ($H_1$): The series is stationary.
Test Results (Table 1):

**Table 1.** Stationarity test results

| Metric | Value |
| --- | --- |
| Test Statistic | −0.987 |
| p-value | 0.754 |
| Critical Value (1%) | −3.538 |
| Stationarity Status(1/0) | 0 |

Conclusion: Since the p-value > 0.05, we accept the null hypothesis, indicating that the series is non-stationary. As the data is non-stationary, we perform first-order differencing.

We conduct first-order differencing using the moving average method and the simple exponential smoothing method:

① Moving Average Method.

By taking the average number of moving terms $N < T$, the moving average method was employed., $T = 12$

$$M_t^{(1)} = \frac{1}{t}(y_t + y_{t+1} + \cdots + y_{t+N-1}) \tag{1}$$

$$\hat{y}_{t+1} = M_t^{(1)} = \frac{1}{t}(\hat{y}_t + \hat{y}_{t+1} + \cdots + \hat{y}_{t+N-1}) \tag{2}$$

② Exponential Smoothing Method.

Single Exponential Smoothing Method: The data exhibits the following characteristics: it undergoes periodic fluctuations and tends to follow a linear trend when special factors are removed.

$$S_t^{(1)} = \alpha y_t + (1-\alpha)S_{t-1}^{(1)} = S_{t-1}^{(1)} + \alpha\left(y_t - S_{t-1}^{(1)}\right) \tag{3}$$

$$M_t^{(1)} = M_{t-1}^{(1)} + \frac{y_t - y_{t-N}}{N} \tag{4}$$

$M_{t-1}^{(1)}$ is the best estimate for $y_{t-N}$,

$$M_t^{(1)} = \frac{y_t}{N} + \left(1 - \frac{1}{N}\right)M_{t-1}^{(1)} \tag{5}$$

Let $\alpha = \frac{1}{N}$, Replace $S_t$ to $M_t^{(1)}$, When expanded, it becomes

$$S_t^{(1)} = \alpha y_t + (1-\alpha)\left[\alpha y_{t-1} + (1-\alpha)S_{t-2}^{(1)}\right] = \alpha \sum_{i=0}^{t}(1-\alpha)^i y_{t-i} \tag{6}$$

The weighted coefficient is $\alpha, \alpha(1-\alpha), \alpha(1-\alpha)^2, \alpha(1-\alpha)^i$, It conforms to the law of weighted coefficients and has the function of smoothing the data.

$$\text{Forecasting Model}: \hat{y}_{t+1} = \alpha y_t + (1-\alpha)\hat{y}_t \tag{7}$$

The sequence after differentiation passes the ADF test (p = 0.000). It becomes stationary (as shown in Fig. 2).

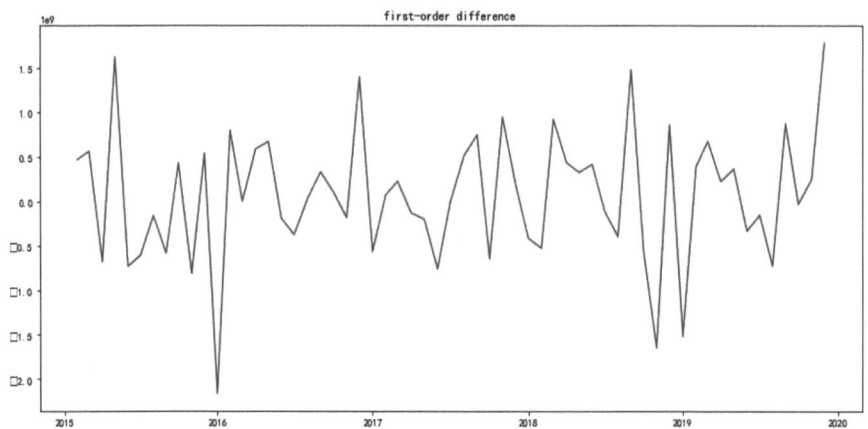

**Fig. 2.** Data smoothing

### 3.1.2 Seasonal Decomposition Model for Time Series

Decompose the sequence into trend (T), seasonal (S) residual (R) components using an additive model:

$$Y_t = Trend_t + Seasonal_t + Residual_t \tag{8}$$

In practical scenarios, multiple rounds of differentiation or seasonal differentiation may be required to ascertain whether the differentiated data is sufficiently stationary. For seasonal decomposition, a 12-month cycle is employed. To ensure the accuracy of the decomposition, this paper adopts a seasonal difference order of D = 1 and a period of 12 in the SARIMAX model to guarantee the stationarity of the residuals.

① Trend modeling method/Linear fitting

This paper employs the least squares method to fit a straight line $\hat{y}_t = a + bt$.

$$\begin{cases} \sum y = na + b \\ \sum ty = a\sum t + b\sum t^2 \end{cases} \tag{9}$$

$$\begin{cases} a = \frac{\sum t^2 \sum y - \sum y \sum yt}{n\sum t^2 - (\sum t)^2} \\ b = \frac{n\sum ty - \sum t \sum y}{n\sum t^2 - (\sum t)^2} \end{cases} \tag{10}$$

The seasonal component exhibits a 12-month periodic pattern, and the residuals pass the ADF test (p < 0.05). Satisfy stationary, as shown in Fig. 3:

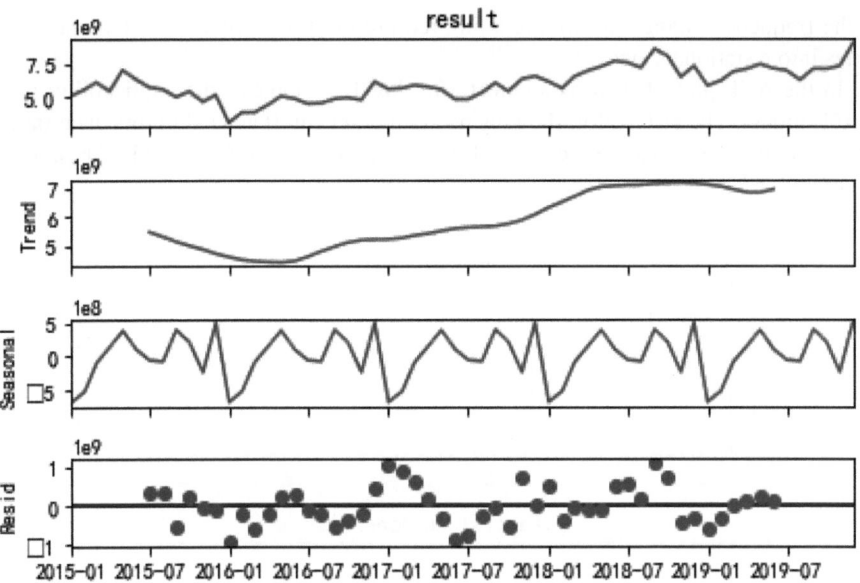

**Fig. 3.** Seasonal decomposition model

### 3.1.3 Model Parameter Selection

Auto-regressive Integrated Moving Average Model ARIMA(p, d, q)

$$W_t^{(d)} = \phi_0 + \phi_1 y_{t-1} + \phi_2 y_{t-2} + \cdots + \phi_p y_{t-p} + \epsilon_t - \epsilon_t \theta_1 y_{t-1} - \theta_2 y_{t-2} - \cdots - \theta_q y_{t-q} \quad (11)$$

Exponential smoothing is highly beneficial for forecasting. In certain scenarios, we can create better forecasting models by considering the correlations among the data. The Auto-regressive Integrated Moving Average Model (ARIMA) incorporates an explicit statistical model to handle the irregular component of a time series, allowing for autocorrelation within the irregular part. For seasonal time series data, the short-term non-seasonal component is likely to contribute to the model. The ARIMA model is typically represented as ARIMA(p, q, d), where:

p is the number of lagged observations used when training the model (i.e., the order of the auto-regressive term).

d is the number of times differences are applied (i.e., the order of differentiating).

q is the size of the moving average window (i.e., the order of the moving average term).

*3.1.3.1 ACF/PACF Analysis* The Auto-correlation Function (ACF) is utilized to calculate the linear correlation between observations in a time series separated by p lags. The Partial Auto-correlation Function (PACF) is employed to determine the number of auto-regressive terms, q, needed. The Inverse Auto-correlation Function (IACF) is used to detect over-differentiating. Subsequently, initial values for the auto-regressive order p, the differentiating order d, the moving average order q, as well as their corresponding seasonal parameters P, D, and Q, can be obtained. The parameter d represents the order of the frequency change in differentiating required to transform a non-stationary time series into a stationary one.

In the ACF plot, if there is a cutoff after lag 1, it suggests the applicability of an MA(1) model. The PACF plot, showing no significant cutoff and exhibiting clear tailing characteristics, rules out the presence of AR components. The ACF and PACF plots are illustrated in Fig. 4.

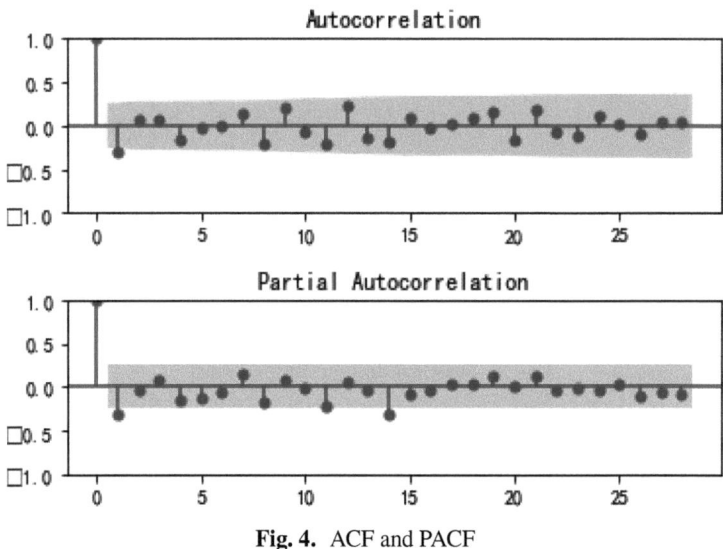

**Fig. 4.** ACF and PACF

Auto-correlation Function (ACF) Plot: It displays the correlation between a time series and its own lagged values. Cutoff: If the ACF abruptly cuts off (approaches zero) after lag q, it indicates the applicability of an MA(q) model. Conversely, if the Partial Auto-correlation Function (PACF) abruptly cuts off after lag p, it suggests the applicability of an AR(p) model. Judgment Rules:

AR(p) Model: The PACF cuts off at lag p, while the ACF trails off.
MA(q) Model: The ACF cuts off at lag q, while the PACF trails off.
ARMA(p,q) Model: Both the ACF and PACF trail off.
Preliminary Parameter Suggestion: ARIMA(0,1,0).

*3.1.3.2 Grid Search Optimization for BIC* Traverse all combinations of p (ranging from 0 to 5) and q (ranging from 0 to 5) to calculate the Bayesian Information Criterion (BIC):

$$BIC = -2 * log - likelihood + k * ln(n) \qquad (12)$$

where $k$ is the number of model parameters, and $n$ is the sample size. A smaller *BIC* value indicates a better model.

*3.1.3.3 Selection of Optimal Parameters* Grid Search Validation: Traverse all possible (p, q) combinations, calculate the BIC, and select the parameters corresponding to the minimum BIC value. The optimal model is identified as ARIMA(0, 1, 0). Note that certain (p, q) combinations may lead to non-convergence, and exceptions should be captured (e.g., using the except clause in code).

Optimal Parameters:

Non-seasonal part: p = 0, q = 0 (corresponding to the minimum BIC value).

Seasonal part: The seasonal order is determined as seasonal_order = (2, 1, 2, 12) through SARIMA grid search (with AIC = 560.85).

The optimization was conducted based on previous research findings, integrating intelligent parameter optimization through grid search and Bayesian criteria. The parameters determined through automated optimization were subsequently utilized to run the previous version of the code, yielding results that aligned with expectations. However, during the execution of the new code version, the grid search process demonstrated considerable time consumption. While performance optimization is planned for future iterations, this thesis provides two distinct code implementations to address this temporal limitation.

### 3.2 Model Construction and Diagnostics

#### 3.2.1 SARIMA Model Fitting

Model Expression:

$SARIMA(0, 1, 0) \times (2, 1, 2)_{12}$

Trend Component Range: 277,568.83.

Seasonal Amplitude: 28,489.35.

Residual Standard Deviation: 49,105.47.

Parameter Estimation Results: Conclusion: All parameters are indicating that the model is valid. See Fig. 5.

```
==============================================================================
                 coef    std err          z      P>|z|      [0.025      0.975]
------------------------------------------------------------------------------
ar.S.L12      -0.4409      3.864     -0.114      0.909      -8.014       7.132
ar.S.L24      -0.3248      0.925     -0.351      0.725      -2.137       1.487
ma.S.L12      -0.0371      3.817     -0.010      0.992      -7.518       7.444
ma.S.L24       0.1326      3.052      0.043      0.965      -5.849       6.114
sigma2       6.712e+09   1.71e-09   3.93e+18     0.000    6.71e+09    6.71e+09
==============================================================================
                                SARIMAX Results
==============================================================================
Dep. Variable:                           y   No. Observations:             60
Model:             SARIMAX(3, 1, 3)x(2, 1, [1, 2], 12)   Log Likelihood  -587.890
Date:                       Mon, 02 Jun 2025   AIC                     1199.781
Time:                               18:22:20   BIC                     1221.983
Sample:                           01-01-2015   HQIC                    1208.135
                                - 12-01-2019
Covariance Type:                         opg
==============================================================================
                 coef    std err          z      P>|z|      [0.025      0.975]
------------------------------------------------------------------------------
intercept    6444.8185   3.49e+04      0.185      0.853   -6.19e+04    7.48e+04
ar.L1          -0.4126      0.925     -0.446      0.655      -2.225       1.400
ar.L2          -0.2738      1.022     -0.268      0.789      -2.277       1.730
ar.L3           0.5263      0.953      0.552      0.581      -1.341       2.394
ma.L1           0.3855      0.835      0.462      0.644      -1.250       2.021
ma.L2           0.1110      0.980      0.113      0.910      -1.810       2.033
ma.L3          -0.7258      0.923     -0.786      0.432      -2.535       1.083
ar.S.L12       -0.6902      3.060     -0.226      0.822      -6.688       5.308
ar.S.L24       -0.4013      1.067     -0.376      0.707      -2.492       1.689
ma.S.L12        0.2077      2.992      0.069      0.945      -5.656       6.071
ma.S.L24        0.0793      2.989      0.027      0.979      -5.779       5.937
sigma2       6.206e+09      0.095    6.56e+10    0.000     6.21e+09    6.21e+09
==============================================================================
Ljung-Box (L1) (Q):                    0.03   Jarque-Bera (JB):            0.00
Prob(Q):                               0.87   Prob(JB):                    1.00
Heteroskedasticity (H):                1.95   Skew:                        0.00
Prob(H) (two-sided):                   0.19   Kurtosis:                    2.96
==============================================================================

=== 网格搜索开始 (贝叶斯BIC准则) ===
▲ 发现更优模型 BIC=1583.81 | 参数 {'D': 0, 'P': 0, 'Q': 0, 'd': 0, 'p': 0, 'q': 0}
▲ 发现更优模型 BIC=1564.66 | 参数 {'D': 0, 'P': 0, 'Q': 0, 'd': 0, 'p': 0, 'q': 1}
▲ 发现更优模型 BIC=1563.34 | 参数 {'D': 0, 'P': 0, 'Q': 0, 'd': 0, 'p': 0, 'q': 2}
▲ 发现更优模型 BIC=1559.13 | 参数 {'D': 0, 'P': 0, 'Q': 0, 'd': 0, 'p': 0, 'q': 3}
▲ 发现更优模型 BIC=1526.95 | 参数 {'D': 0, 'P': 0, 'Q': 0, 'd': 0, 'p': 1, 'q': 0}
▲ 发现更优模型 BIC=1499.88 | 参数 {'D': 0, 'P': 0, 'Q': 0, 'd': 1, 'p': 0, 'q': 0}
▲ 发现更优模型 BIC=1279.70 | 参数 {'D': 1, 'P': 0, 'Q': 0, 'd': 0, 'p': 0, 'q': 0}
▲ 发现更优模型 BIC=1269.71 | 参数 {'D': 1, 'P': 0, 'Q': 0, 'd': 0, 'p': 0, 'q': 1}
▲ 发现更优模型 BIC=1267.33 | 参数 {'D': 1, 'P': 0, 'Q': 0, 'd': 0, 'p': 0, 'q': 2}
▲ 发现更优模型 BIC=1255.74 | 参数 {'D': 1, 'P': 0, 'Q': 0, 'd': 0, 'p': 3, 'q': 1}
▲ 发现更优模型 BIC=1206.51 | 参数 {'D': 1, 'P': 0, 'Q': 0, 'd': 1, 'p': 0, 'q': 0}
▲ 发现更优模型 BIC=1195.56 | 参数 {'D': 1, 'P': 0, 'Q': 1, 'd': 1, 'p': 0, 'q': 0}

=== 最优模型 ===
参数: {'D': 1, 'P': 0, 'Q': 1, 'd': 1, 'p': 0, 'q': 0} | BIC=1195.56
```

**Fig. 5.** Parameter Estimation Results

### 3.2.2 Model Diagnostics

Residual Normality: The Q-Q plot indicates that the residuals approximate a normal distribution.

Residual Auto-correlation: The Ljung-Box test ($p > 0.05$) suggests that the residuals exhibit white noise characteristics (Fig. 6).

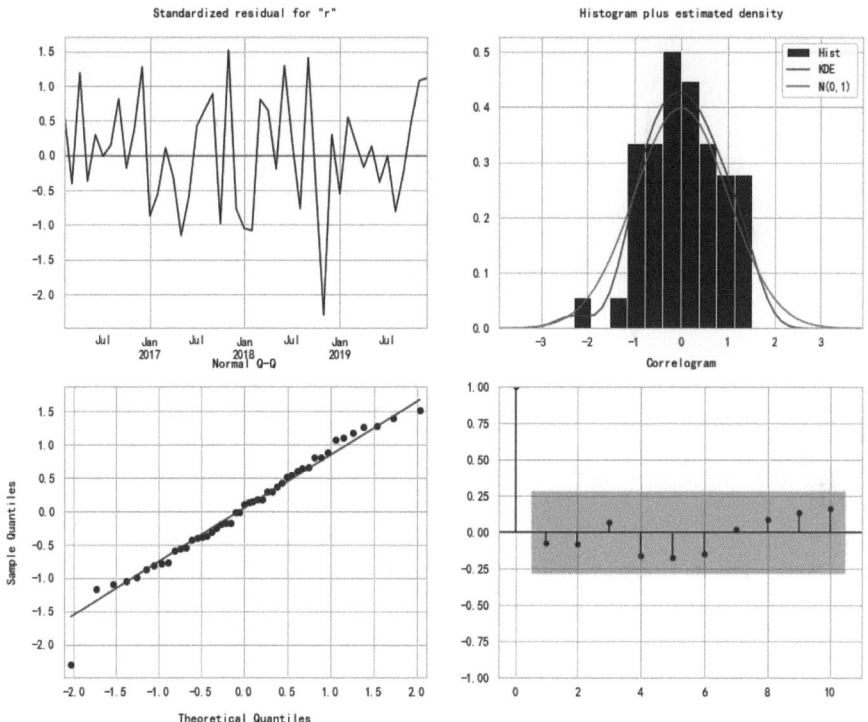

**Fig. 6.** Model Diagnostics Parameters

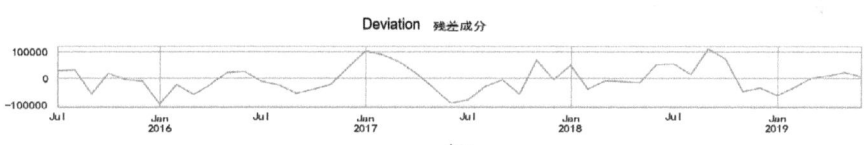

**Fig. 7.** Residual Standard Deviation

Forecast Comparison: The comparison between forecast values and actual values demonstrates a good fit (RMSE = 115124) (Figs. 7, 8, 9, 10).

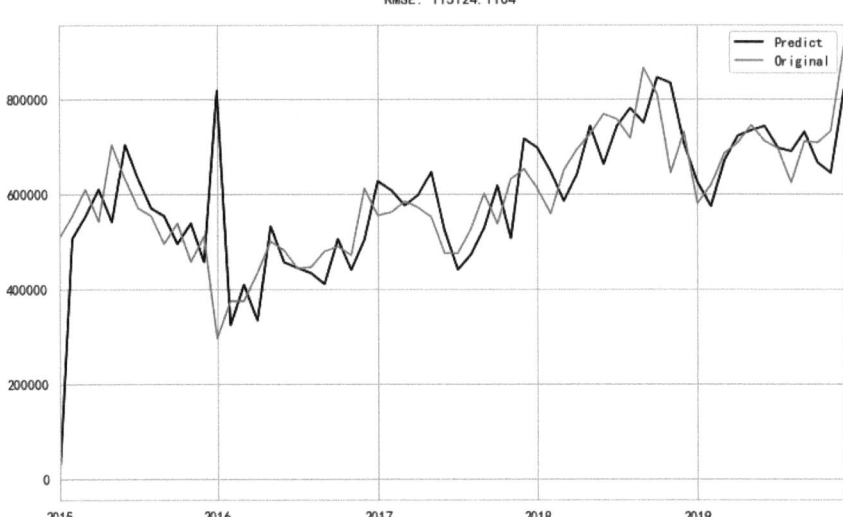

**Fig. 8.** Comparison Results Between Forecasts and Actual Values

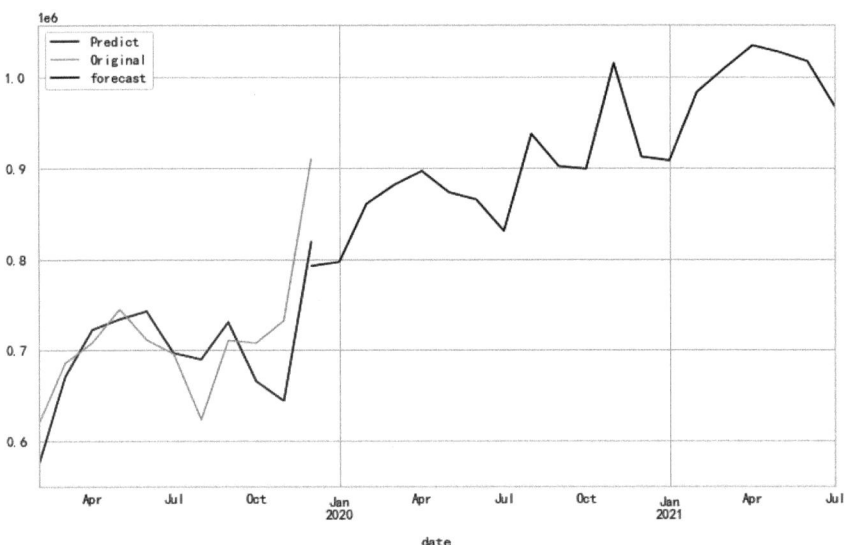

**Fig. 9.** Forecast outcomes for the subsequent 20 months

**Fig. 10.** Model test and Forecast outcomes

### 3.3 Effectiveness of the Methodology:

① Standardization Processing: First-order differentiating successfully eliminated the trend, with the ADF test serving as the core tool in the Standardization process.
② Seasonal Modeling: SARIMA, with a seasonal_order of (2, 1, 2, 12), effectively captured the annual cycle, offering advantages over traditional ARIMA models.
③ Parameter Optimization: BIC grid search avoided the risks associated with subjective parameter setting, ensuring the optimal model configuration.

### 3.4 Limitations and Directions for Improvement

① Data Length Limitation: The data-set spanning only 60 months may affect the identification of long-term seasonal patterns.
② Absence of Exogenous Variables: The impact of external factors (such as policies, economic indicators) on the time series was not considered.
③ Model Complexity: Given the relatively large number of parameters in SARIMA, there is a need to be cautious about the risk of over-fitting. Robustness can be further enhanced through rolling forecast cross-validation.
④ Additionally, incorporating the LSTM algorithm with consideration for both short-term and long-term cycles can further optimize the model and improve forecasting accuracy.

Employ a more systematic grid search approach to select the p, d, q parameters, as well as the seasonal P, D, Q parameters, rather than merely fixing PDQ = [0,1,0]. For instance, utilize the auto_arima function to automatically select the optimal parameter combination. Cross-validation: Employ time series cross-validation to evaluate the model's predictive performance and adjust parameters to mitigate over-fitting.

## 4 Conclusion: Future Research Directions

This hybrid framework boosts revenue forecast accuracy and robustness by integrating dynamic feature engineering with an enhanced SARIMA model. It overcomes traditional SARIMA's limitations in handling nonlinear dynamics within complex systems like energy markets. Future extensibility to LSTM-Transformers could capture long-term dependencies. However, given economic uncertainties and diverse data, rigorous sensitivity and robustness testing remain vital. Future research can build on these foundations:

Deep Integration of Dynamic External Factors.

Extract policy/sentiment features via NLP; dynamically weight external variables using attention mechanisms; simulate impact pathways with reinforcement learning.

Lightweight Real-time Optimization.

Enable edge deployment via model compression (knowledge distillation/pruning); implement incremental learning for online updates; enhance multi-step forecasts with Seq2Seq-Monte Carlo integration.

Interpretability & Strategic Synergy.

Identify drivers using causal models (Bayesian networks/SEM); link predictions to operations via dynamic knowledge graphs; develop interactive platforms for scenario simulation.

Cross-domain Generalization Validation.

Reduce retraining costs via cross-industry transfer learning; validate impacts of macroeconomic variables with global data; stress-test robustness against black swan events.

Ethical-Compliance Frameworks.

Detect/correct algorithmic bias; ensure security via federated learning/differential privacy; automate ESG compliance through regulatory knowledge bases.

As the cornerstone of enterprise value chain analysis, the innovation in revenue forecasting methodologies has always been closely intertwined with the complexity of business practices. The hybrid model proposed in this paper represents a significant step forward in enhancing forecasting accuracy. However, in the face of dynamic environments and diversified demands, continuous breakthroughs are still needed in areas such as external factor modeling, real-time deployment, and interpretability enhancement. Future research should deeply integrate multidisciplinary perspectives from data science, operations research, and social sciences to drive the paradigm shift of predictive models from being merely "precise tools" to becoming "intelligent decision-making partners," thereby injecting algorithmic momentum into the sustainable development of global enterprises.

Attachment 1: Source Code and Data Set: (Keep 30 days).
Data:factor.csv.
Link: https://pan.baidu.com/s/1hvtEB-vbdDLuvoB1THivpQ.
Access code: uk5z.
Version 1 Source code: factor_20250429_1939_py.
Link: https://pan.baidu.com/s/1fHZ-LawCXrOAApW9c6-USw.
Access code: u29s.
Version 2 Source code: factor_20250602_1817.py.
Link: https://pan.baidu.com/s/1pqL0eRT6CvpZ7moPw_rNfA.
Access code: 33cz.

# References

1. Zhang, Y., Li, T., Wang, Q.: Limitations of traditional time series models in revenue forecasting under policy shocks. J. Financ. Anal. **15**(3), 45–60 (2021)
2. Ye, Q.: An empirical study on the influencing factors of regional Gross Domestic Product (GDP) - Based on Multiple Regression Analysis. Hans Publishers(Hans Publishers) (2023). https://www.hanspub.org/journal/paperinformation?paperid=76424
3. Qian, L., et al.: Transformer for Non-Autoregressive Neural Machine Translation [EB/OL]. arXiv, 13 May 2021. https://arxiv.org/abs/2008.07905
4. Heaton, J.: Artificial Intelligence Algorithms (Volumes 1–5), 1st edn. Translated by Li Erchao. Beijing: Posts & Telecom Press (2020)
5. Zhang, H., Wang, L.: Research on supply chain management based on LSTM. Comput. Eng. Appl. **56**(4), 127–132 (2020)
6. Zhang, L., Li, M.: Research on stock price prediction model based on LSTM. Comput. Appl. Res. **36**(1), 123–127 (2019)
7. Li, H., Zhang, Z.: Deep learning and time series forecasting. Comput. Sci. **46**(1), 1–10 (2019)
8. Zhang, Y., Li, T., Wang, Q.: Research on the Limitations of Enterprise Revenue Forecasting Models under Policy Shocks. Economic Science Press, Beijing (2021)
9. Guo, L., Zhou, M., Liu, X.: Long-term Revenue Forecasting Based on a Hybrid Transformer-LSTM Model. Zhejiang University Press, Hangzhou (2024)
10. Cho, K., et al.: Learning Phrase Representations using RNN Encoder-Decoder for Statistical Machine Translation. arXiv preprint arXiv:1406.1078 (2014)
11. Sutskever, I., Vinyals, O., Le, Q.V.: Sequence to sequence learning with neural networks. Adv. Neural. Inf. Process. Syst. **27**, 3104–3112 (2014)
12. Hochreiter, S., Schmidhuber, J.: Long short-term memory. Neural Comput. **9**(8), 1735–1780 (1997)
13. Bayer, J., Osendorfer, C., van der Smagt, P.: Learning Sequence Representations. arXiv preprint arXiv:1502.01852 (2015)
14. Box, G.E.P., Jenkins, G.M., Reinsel, G.C.: Time Series Analysis: Forecasting and Control. Wiley (2015)
15. Hyndman, R. J., Athanasopoulos, G.: Forecasting: Principles and Practice. OTexts (2021)
16. Zhang C.: Financial Time Series Analysis. Tsinghua University Press (2018)

# A Microservice-Based Implementation of Chinese Conversational Digital Avatars Using NVIDIA ACE

FuChe Wu[1]([✉]) [iD], KuoHsiung Chen[2], and Andrew Dellinger[3] [iD]

[1] Providence University, Taichung, Taiwan
`fcwu@gm.pu.edu.tw`
[2] MagV Co, Ltd., Taipei, Taiwan
`victor@magv.com`
[3] Elon University, Elon, USA
`adellinger@elon.edu`

**Abstract.** This paper presents implementing a Chinese conversational digital avatar system based on NVIDIA ACE (Avatar Cloud Engine). The system enables modular expansion and customization according to diverse application requirements by leveraging the highly flexible microservice architecture of NVIDIA ACE, combined with Kubernetes cluster management. We construct a Chinese speech interaction pipeline on this foundation, integrating modules for automatic speech recognition, natural language understanding, text-to-speech synthesis, and facial animation, thereby achieving a product-level virtual avatar solution. There are different workflows in ACE 4.1 Omniverse Rendering, Unreal Rendering, and the latest 5.0 architecture, and we compare the differences in realism, interactivity, and development flexibility among these rendering technologies during implementation. Experimental results demonstrate that the NVIDIA ACE architecture offers high scalability and stability, allowing seamless integration of third-party Chinese speech and language models to enhance Chinese virtual avatars' interaction quality and application scope. This study focuses on system integration and productization experience, elaborates on the challenges encountered and solutions adopted during development, and provides a reference for future development and deployment of Chinese conversational avatar applications.

**Keywords:** Virtual Avatar · Large Language Model(LLM) · Automatic Speech Recognition(ASR) · Text-to-speech(TTS)

## 1 Introduction

Humans have always been a central research focus, and the creation of realistic virtual humans or talking avatars has long been a significant topic. In recent

---

This work was supported by the National Science and Technology Council, Taiwan, R.O.C., under grant no. NSTC 113-2221-E-126-007.

years, with the advent of large language models (LLMs), the development of real-time, interactive virtual characters has become an increasingly important application.

NVIDIA ACE (Avatar Cloud Engine) is a real-time AI solution that supports end-to-end development of large-scale interactive virtual humans and digital human applications. Its customizable microservice architecture, built on NVIDIA's Unified Compute Services, a full-stack AI platform, and RTX technology, provides the industry's fastest and most flexible solution for building virtual humans. Developers can leverage ACE to seamlessly integrate NVIDIA AI capabilities into their applications, including Riva speech and translation AI, Voice Font (for creating digital voice clones), NeMo LLM (for natural language understanding), Audio2Emotion, Animation Graph, Omniverse Renderer, and A2F-2D or A2F-3D (AI-driven 2D/3D character animation) modules. The NVIDIA ACE Tokkio architecture is a highly flexible, high-performance solution for building avatars.

The system architecture of NVIDIA ACE Tokkio, is specifically designed to address the various challenges of virtual human applications, including speech, language, animation, real-time performance, and scalability. According to official documentation, Tokkio uses a distributed, event-driven microservice architecture to support real-time virtual human interaction through multiple parallel processing pipelines. The system operates from the front-end web UI or application, transmitting user speech and video data to the back end via WebRTC and WebSocket. The backend streaming pipeline communicates and manages media streams, ensuring that audio and video are delivered with low latency and high stability, thus laying a solid foundation for real-time interaction.

This layered microservice architecture loosely couples advanced speech, language, and animation technologies and leverages Kubernetes to provide a stable, scalable, and highly modular platform for building digital virtual humans. Whether in speech recognition, semantic understanding, real-time interaction, animation synchronization, or system scalability, the design of NVIDIA ACE Tokkio effectively addresses the challenges faced by Chinese virtual human applications, providing a solid foundation for the deployment and large-scale development of Chinese virtual human technologies.

## 2 Previous Work

In recent years, the development of virtual avatar technology has accelerated, primarily driven by the demand for real-time interaction and high realism. Early virtual avatars mainly adopted animation-based approaches, decomposing 2D or 3D images into different parts and animating them through event-driven mechanisms. Tools such as Live2D are representative of this technique, particularly suitable for anime-style characters. However, while this approach is mature, achieving a high degree of realism is difficult. With the advent of generative models, especially technologies like Stable Diffusion, the quality of virtual avatars has improved significantly. However, real-time interaction remains limited by the substantial computational resources required.

The core of generative virtual avatar technology lies in the evolution of 3D reconstruction and rendering methods. Neural Radiance Fields (NeRF) [10] represents a breakthrough, enabling the generation of high-quality 3D scenes from a small number of 2D images, thus revolutionizing virtual avatar modeling. To accelerate NeRF rendering, Tri-plane NeRF [2] and its partitioned variants decompose 3D space into multiple planes, significantly improving generation speed and making it suitable for real-time applications. The partitioned tri-plane method further divides scenes or objects into regions, each represented by three planes, enhancing rendering flexibility and efficiency. Recently, Gaussian Splatting techniques [3,8,13,18] approximate 3D scenes with Gaussian point clouds, further improving real-time rendering efficiency and becoming the foundation for many contemporary studies. For example, GaussianTalker [3] leverages the fast rendering capability of 3D Gaussian Splatting, fusing 3D Gaussian attributes with audio features to achieve real-time, controllable talking face synthesis. Ma et al. [8] use 3D Gaussian blend shapes to represent head animation, combining a neutral head model with expression blend shapes to generate accurate virtual avatars with arbitrary expressions. Qian et al. [13] combine the SMPL model with LBS techniques, binding details such as clothing and hair to the skeleton and modeling dynamic attributes using Gaussian point clouds. Xu et al. [18] propose a Gaussian Parametric Head Model, enabling precise control of identity and expression, and design a comprehensive training framework to ensure convergence and detail fidelity.

The history of 3D virtual avatar modeling is long, evolving from skeleton-driven deformation to blend shape techniques, gradually enhancing the granularity of expressions and movements. The 52 blend shapes defined by Apple have become an industry standard, while NVIDIA's Audio2Face technology can convert speech into corresponding expression weights, enabling speech-driven facial animation. With its maturity and efficiency, traditional mesh rendering remains the mainstream choice for real-time applications on mobile devices, while neural texture and Unet-based methods further improve texture consistency and detail restoration. For example, Basbirov et al. [1] first identify matching meshes and then train global neural textures, achieving real-time re-rendering via UNet. Pavlakos et al. [11] propose the SMPL-X parametric model, which can build universal meshes matching images and support 3D capture of hands, faces, and bodies.

Although NeRF and its derivatives can reconstruct highly realistic 3D scenes, most methods are only suitable for static objects, and handling dynamic expressions and head movements remains challenging. Park et al. [10] propose Nerfies, which record non-static information as continuous MLP functions for deformation and train the model from coarse to fine, achieving realistic reconstruction of deformable scenes. Gafni et al. [4] train head shape, color, expression coefficients, and per-frame implicit codes into a dynamic neural radiance field. Zhuang et al. [24] input facial shape, expression, appearance, spatial coordinates, and view direction into an MLP to generate photorealistic images, with RefineNet used for detail enhancement. Wangbo et al. [22] use 3D GAN priors and design an efficient encoder-decoder network to reconstruct the neural volume of the source image, proposing a compensation network to supplement facial details and achieve fine-grained dynamic control. Wang et al. [17] obtain pose and expression parameters via 3DMM, combine them with StyleGAN to generate foreground, background, and final composites, and emphasize the importance of pixel alignment for UNet-based generation.

For dynamic expressions and speech-driven animation, Li et al. [7] propose a NeRF-based tri-plane hash representation, using a regional attention module to associate audio features with spatial regions and capture local motion priors, enabling speech-driven lip generation. Shen et al. [14] propose Dynamic Facial Radiance Fields (DFRF), which can quickly generalize to new identities with limited training data and learn facial priors via facial radiance fields. Shen et al. [15] further propose DiffTalk, combining audio synthesis with facial landmarks to generate high-quality, personalized talking heads with elegant support for high-resolution output. Peng et al. [12] emphasize the synchronized coordination of subject identity, lip motion, facial expression, and head pose, inputting all these data into the tri-plane to enhance the realism of talking faces. Ye et al. [21] propose MimicTalk, which requires only 15 min to learn the personalized static appearance and facial dynamic features through a static-dynamic hybrid adaptation process and introduce a stylized audio-to-motion model to mimic the speaking style in reference videos.

For 3D structure and representation, Chan et al. [2] were the first to apply tri-plane to 3D facial structure synthesis, initiating a series of related studies. Sun et al. [16] propose Generative Texture-Rasterized Tri-planes, combining mesh-guided explicit deformation with implicit volumetric representation, achieving fine expression control and topological flexibility. Ma et al. [9] invert portrait images into identity codes, combine them with motion codes to generate tri-plane volumes, and use volumetric Rendering to create images from arbitrary viewpoints. Zhao et al. [23] process the head and body separately, training fusion weights to combine renderings and solve the problem of differing head and body poses. Grassal et al. [6] use the FLAME controllable model as a basis, training a displacement network to simulate hair and material space, generating the surface geometry and appearance of virtual avatars.

Additionally, Giebenhain et al. [5] use a neural parametric head model (NPHM), conditioning dynamic appearance on NPHM's rich expression space and converting inverse deformation fields into forward deformation fields compatible with rasterized Rendering, with remaining details learned from multi-view videos. Xu et al. [19,20] propose AvatarMAV and LatentAvatar, respectively; the former quickly converge in a 4D model after obtaining different expressions via 3DMM, while the latter uses tri-plane to learn the presentation of different expressions and emphasizes joint feature learning and high-resolution generation.

Virtual avatar technology has evolved from traditional animation-based approaches to diverse architectures combining generative models, 3D reconstruction, and efficient Rendering. These technological breakthroughs have enabled virtual avatars to achieve unprecedented realism and real-time interactivity in applications such as gaming, interactive education, and virtual performances, striking a good balance between image quality and efficiency. The aforementioned research and technological developments lay a solid foundation for the real-time generation and personalized interaction of future virtual avatars.

## 3 Differences Between Omniverse Rendering and Unreal Rendering

Within the NVIDIA ACE architecture, Omniverse Render and Unreal Rendering differ significantly in terms of technical positioning, integration methods, rendering quality, and application flexibility. For practical web deployment and server-side Audio2Face rendering, currently only the integration of Omniverse and Unreal with the Pixel Streaming server is mature and well-supported. Therefore, this paper focuses on these two frameworks. We have also conducted preliminary experiments with Unity and web-based frontends, but at present, they can only obtain blendshape parameters via the NIM API. While this approach is less refined in terms of visual quality, it offers the advantage of significantly reducing GPU costs.

Omniverse Render is a core component of the NVIDIA Omniverse ecosystem, designed for highly realistic, physically accurate 3D scene rendering and multi-user collaboration. It is deeply integrated with AI microservices such as Audio2Face, enabling real-time facial animation of virtual avatars driven by speech. It uses USD (Universal Scene Description) as the standard format for scene and animation exchange. Omniverse Render supports RTX real-time ray and path tracing, delivering high-quality lighting, materials, and details. It is particularly suitable for applications requiring high realism, AI-driven animation, and multi-department collaboration, such as digital twins, visual effects for film, and industrial design. Its advantages include seamless integration with other NVIDIA AI microservices (such as Audio2Face and Animation Graph) and the ability to perform distributed Rendering and collaboration on cloud or local GPUs.

On the other hand, Unreal Rendering is based on Epic Games' Unreal Engine, emphasizing real-time interaction, gamified experiences, and highly programmable content creation. In the ACE architecture, Unreal Rendering primarily uses Pixel Streaming technology to stream Unreal Engine-rendered 3D scenes in real time to front-end browsers or devices. Unreal Engine excels at handling complex scene logic, character animation, physical simulation, and visual effects and boasts a rich ecosystem of development tools and resources. It is especially suitable for scenarios requiring high interactivity, gamified workflows, or immersive experiences, such as virtual exhibitions, digital tours, and interactive games. Unreal Rendering within the ACE framework can also be integrated with speech, language, and animation microservices. Still, animation driving and rendering quality are adjusted according to the features and resources of Unreal Engine.

In summary, ACE Omniverse Render focuses on high quality, physical realism, and AI animation integration, making it suitable for applications that demand realism and professional collaboration. In contrast, ACE Unreal Rendering emphasizes real-time interaction, gamified experiences, and development flexibility, making it ideal for scenarios requiring rich interactivity and rapid content production. Both can work in concert with ACE's speech, language, and animation microservices, but the choice of rendering technology depends on your application requirements, target experience, and development resources.

Omniverse Render adopts USD (Universal Scene Description) as the standard format for scenes and animations, which is very developer-friendly. Since USD is designed for programmable and extensible 3D data exchange, developers can directly read, write, and modify USD files using Python or C++, flexibly controlling scene content, animation parameters, and character details. This high degree of programmability allows nearly all rendering, animation, and scene logic requirements to be implemented programmatically, whether for automated workflows, batch content generation, or deep integration with AI microservices. However, this also means that many details require developers to write code themselves. For teams lacking 3D programming experience, the learning curve is steep, and the production process is relatively primitive, lacking a complete visual toolchain and content resources.

In contrast, Unreal Engine offers a much more refined production workflow. It comes with the built-in Metahuman system, allowing developers to quickly create highly realistic, animatable virtual characters through a graphical interface, with direct support for skeletal animation, facial expressions, and physical simulation. This dramatically lowers the barrier to content creation, enabling designers without programming backgrounds to participate in virtual human development easily. The rich resource ecosystem of Unreal provides many ready-to-use animations, effects, and scenes, resulting in high development efficiency and suitability for rapid iteration and large-scale content production. However, for highly customized development or deep integration with external AI systems, there may be limitations imposed by the Engine's architecture.

In summary, the USD file format and programmability of Omniverse Render provide developers with exceptional flexibility and control, making it suitable for professional applications requiring fine-tuning and automated workflows. Unreal Engine, on the other hand, with its comprehensive content production tools and resource ecosystem, makes virtual human development faster and more accessible, especially for teams seeking high efficiency and visual operation. Each has its advantages, and the choice should be made based on the team's technical background and the project's needs. The main differences between Omniverse ACE Render and Unreal Engine are summarized in Table 1.

Our production process begins with using a 3D scanner to capture a real person's 3D model and corresponding texture maps, as illustrated in Fig. 1. These assets are then imported into Unreal Engine's Metahuman system for further refinement, such as adding hair, eyes, teeth, tongue, and other features to enhance the realism and completeness of the virtual character.

However, when exporting these characters in USD (Universal Scene Description) format, we often encounter difficulties, especially in handling hair materials.

**Table 1.** Comparison between Omniverse ACE Render and Unreal Engine

| Item | Omniverse ACE Render | Unreal Engine |
| --- | --- | --- |
| Supported ACE version | 4.1 only | 4.1 and 5.0 |
| MetaHuman integration | Difficult | Seamless |
| Voice control support | Yes | Yes |
| Visual fidelity (hair) | Poor (hair material issues) | Excellent |

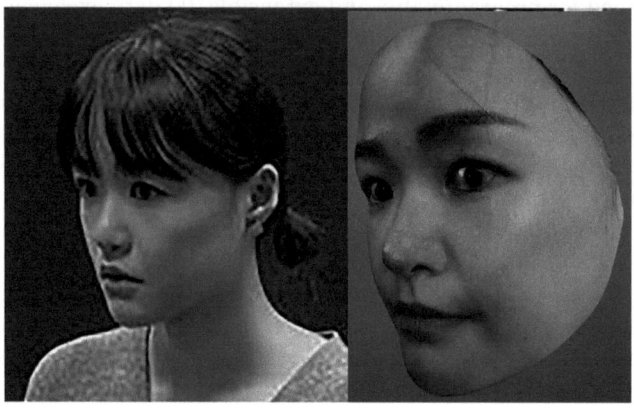

**Fig. 1.** 3D scanning of a person for model acquisition.

This may be related to shader settings for hair, transparency handling, or material compatibility between Metahuman and the USD format. Due to our limited experience in this area, hair materials often do not appear as expected after export, which is a significant challenge in our current workflow.

In contrast, rendering directly within Unreal Engine or integrating with the Metahuman system is relatively easy and stable. Unreal's strong support for Metahuman ensures smooth integration and Rendering of materials, skeletons, and animations, which is why many projects currently choose Unreal as the final presentation platform. The result is shown in Fig. 2.

In summary, while 3D scanning combined with Metahuman can significantly enhance the realism of virtual characters, handling details-especially hair materials—during cross-platform or cross-format (such as USD) export still requires more experience and technical refinement. Further research and optimization in this area will help improve the usability and consistency of virtual characters across multiple platforms.

Fig. 2. final presentation.

## 4 Differences Between Version 4.1 and 5.0

In ACE version 4.1, system functionalities such as automatic speech recognition (ASR), text-to-speech (TTS), and large language models (LLM) are all deployed as independent microservices. The collaboration among these services mainly relies on a controller, which coordinates the operation of each service based on events, integrating processes such as speech, language, and animation to provide a unified virtual human service externally. However, the controller in version 4.1 is proprietary and closed-source, which often limits developers in customization or extension, restricting flexibility within the original architecture. Overall, while version 4.1 achieves distributed deployment and event coordination of microservices, the controller layer remains closed and difficult to extend, making it more suitable for applications that follow the official workflow, such as English-based conversations.

In ACE version 5.0, this aspect has changed significantly. The previously closed controller architecture has been fully opened and replaced with an event-driven framework based on pipecat. The Pipecat framework is open-source and highly modular, allowing developers to adjust pipeline processes freely, plugin or remove different AI microservices, and integrate third-party speech, language, or animation services as needed. This design greatly enhances the system's scalability and flexibility, enabling developers to customize and optimize for different application scenarios rapidly. Version 5.0 emphasizes loose coupling, scalability, and ease of integration and customization, supporting larger-scale and more complex virtual human applications and significantly improving development and operational efficiency.

In version 4.1, the system offers many possibilities for integrated applications, especially in multimedia expansion. In addition to speech input and output, version 4.1 also supports video input, allowing virtual avatars to interact with speech and real video content. For example, avatars can respond to facial expressions and movements detected in real-time video, further enhancing the realism and immersion of interactions. This multimodal integration brings more diverse application scenarios for virtual avatars, such as remote teaching, virtual meetings, and online performances. However, such multimedia integration also increases the complexity of the system architecture, requiring handling of video streaming, synchronization of multiple sensor data, real-time analysis, and feedback, all of which pose significant challenges to system stability and performance. Therefore, in version 5.0, the official design no longer includes dedicated video processing features, greatly simplifying the system architecture and focusing on speech and text interaction. While this reduces the flexibility of multimedia interaction, it also makes the system easier to deploy and maintain, lowering the barriers to development and operation.

In summary, the multimedia integration in version 4.1 brings more innovative application possibilities for avatar interaction and increases system complexity. Version 5.0 allows developers to focus more on implementing core functionalities by removing unnecessary components. Each design approach has advantages and disadvantages, and the choice should be made based on actual application needs.

In the official MetaHuman speech interaction workflow, English ASR (Automatic Speech Recognition) and TTS (Text-to-Speech) are primarily supported. A series of complex conversion processes is required to support new languages (such as Chinese). For example, with NVIDIA's speech technology, a standard speech model must first be converted to NeMo format and then further converted to Riva format before it can be used in Riva speech services. This process is complicated and presents a high technical barrier for developers.

To simplify this process, we adopted a different approach: directly utilizing the browser's speech recognition function to obtain transcribed text, which is then sent to the server for semantic processing by a large language model (LLM) and subsequently passed to the controller. The controller then calls our preprepared TTS service to convert Chinese text to speech and drive the virtual avatar's facial expressions simultaneously. We use ElevenLabs' cloud service for TTS, which significantly reduces the complexity of local model conversion and deployment.

However, we also encountered many challenges during implementation. For example, with NVIDIA Riva 4.1, although the official documentation mentions support for custom languages, there are no clear instructions, and related documentation and code samples are limited. After extensive exploration and experimentation, we discovered that the NLP microservice can achieve custom language TTS functionality. This process is much more difficult and lacks guidance compared to the openness of ACE 5.0.

In summary, while the official speech interaction workflow provides comprehensive support for English, expanding to other languages (such as Chinese) requires significant time and effort, whether for model format conversion or API integration. By combining browser-based speech recognition with cloud TTS services, we bypassed some technical barriers, but this also highlights the current shortcomings and areas for improvement in multilingual support on existing speech platforms.

## 5 Implementation and Results

In designing and applying real-time interactive virtual avatar systems, two key user experience indicators are paramount: system response time (latency) and the naturalness and realism of the avatar's presentation. First, response time directly affects the smoothness and immersion of the interaction. Excessive latency can make the interaction feel unnatural and even discourage user engagement, Whether speech recognition, speech synthesis, or real-time driving of facial expressions and movements. This is why, in our workflow design, we strive to simplify the speech processing pipeline. For example, we utilize browser-based speech recognition to reduce model conversion and cloud API calls. We also select efficient TTS services like ElevenLabs to ensure the fastest possible speech feedback.

Second, the virtual avatar's naturalness and realism determine the interaction's authenticity and appeal. This includes the naturalness of the speech and the expression of emotional intonation, as well as the coordination of facial expressions, lip movements, and head motions. To achieve this, we combine 3D scanning, MetaHuman detail enhancement, and speech-driven expression control to make every avatar reaction closely resemble real human behavior. Technically, this involves high-quality 3D modeling, fine material processing, and synchronized generation of speech and facial expressions. Although there are challenges in cross-platform scenarios (such as USD format export), the integration within Unreal Engine has already achieved high realism. As shown in Fig. 3, the avatar exhibits different facial expressions at various moments during speech, demonstrating the naturalness and synchronization of speech-driven animation.

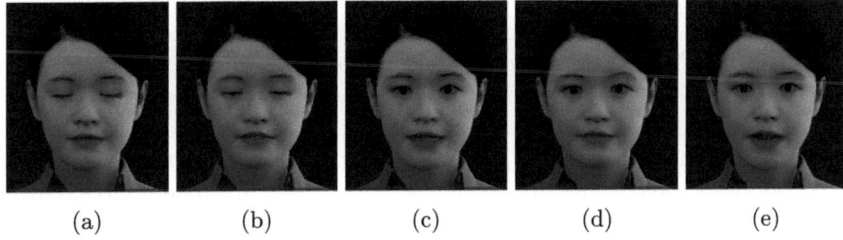

(a)    (b)    (c)    (d)    (e)

**Fig. 3.** Examples of avatar facial expressions at different moments during speech.

Finally, operational cost is also a critical factor for large-scale system deployment. High-quality real-time interactive systems often require substantial computational resources, whether local GPUs, cloud API services (such as ElevenLabs TTS), or high-bandwidth network connections, all contributing to ongoing operational expenses. Furthermore, supporting multilingual or multimodal (e.g., video, speech, motion) integration significantly increases development and maintenance complexity. For example, with NVIDIA Riva, model format conversion, API integration, and lack of clear documentation add to labor and time costs. In contrast, version 5.0 simplifies the system, which, while reducing multimedia interaction flexibility, also effectively lowers maintenance overhead.

Balancing response speed, naturalness, and operational cost is key to designing real-time interactive virtual avatar systems. In the future, further optimizing the synchronization of speech and facial expression generation, improving the convenience of multilingual support, and reducing computational and maintenance costs will help promote the widespread adoption and application of virtual avatars in more domains.

In our experiments, we conducted detailed performance tests on the Chinese virtual avatar system based on the NVIDIA ACE architecture and analyzed the time consumption of each processing stage. The experimental environment used a Google Cloud L4 virtual machine with 4 GPUs, 48 vCPUs, and 192GB of memory. The results showed that the official default all-English conversation workflow was the most fluent, requiring only about three seconds on average to complete a response. This is mainly due to the high degree of optimization for English speech and language models and the streamlined service integration process.

In our custom implementation of version 4.1, speech recognition is performed directly on the browser side, and the recognized text is then sent to the server for semantic processing and response generation. Although this design omits server-side speech recognition, network transmission and server-side processing are still required, resulting in an average response time of about four seconds. For version 5.0, due to its more modular pipeline architecture, data must be transmitted between multiple microservices, and the startup, scheduling, and resource allocation of each service introduce additional latency, extending the overall response time to nearly five seconds.

Further analysis of the time consumption in each processing stage reveals that LLM (large language model) queries take about two seconds on average. In comparison, TTS (text-to-speech) takes about one second. These two steps together account for approximately three seconds of processing time. The total response time naturally increases when adding speech recognition, data transmission, and service integration. This indicates that semantic understanding and speech synthesis are the main performance bottlenecks in Chinese virtual avatar systems.

Regarding GPU usage, in our current experimental environment, following official recommendations, we used a configuration of four Google Cloud L4 GPUs. Tests demonstrated that this setup could reliably support three users interacting simultaneously, with moderate system load and satisfactory GPU utilization, as illustrated in Fig. 4. This demonstrates that L4 GPUs perform very well for real-time Chinese virtual avatar dialogue tasks. However, it is worth noting that GPU resources are considered strategic assets on cloud platforms and are not always

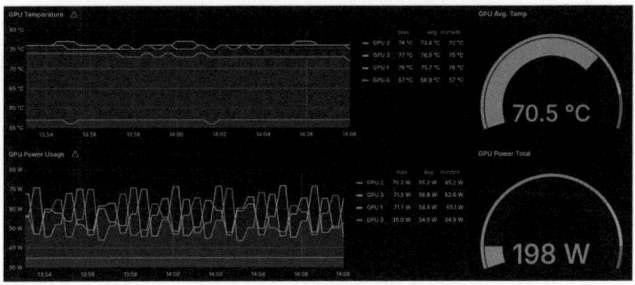

**Fig. 4.** GPU utilization.

easy to obtain. Based on personal experience, lower-end T4 GPUs are often difficult to secure during peak hours (such as evenings). While L4 GPUs offer better performance, the cost of running them continuously is relatively high—about four US dollars per hour—making long-term operation quite expensive.

Therefore, balancing service quality and economic efficiency becomes crucial for large-scale system deployment. Several strategies can be considered to improve cost-effectiveness in the future. For example, dynamically adjusting the number of GPU instances based on user activity, automatically releasing some resources during off-peak hours to reduce idle costs, using lower-end GPU models for non-real-time tasks and reserving high-performance resources for peak-time real-time interaction services, or evaluating the feasibility of hybrid cloud or on-premises GPU deployment, purchasing dedicated hardware for long-term stable service needs to reduce cloud rental costs. Finally, continuously optimizing model performance and system architecture to increase the number of users served per GPU is also a key direction for improving economic efficiency. Achieving the optimal balance among performance, cost, and resource availability will remain a critical consideration and practice for future deployment and expansion of Chinese virtual avatar services.

Table 2 presents a comparison of processing times and GPU usage for ACE v4.1, v5.0, and our custom workflow.

**Table 2.** Comparison of processing time and GPU usage for different workflows

| Item | ACE v4.1 (official) | ACE v5.0 (official) | Custom Workflow |
| --- | --- | --- | --- |
| ASR | ~0.5 s | ~0.5 s | Browser-based, negligible |
| LLM | ~2.0 s | ~2.0 s | ~2.0 s |
| TTS | ~1.0 s | ~1.0 s | ~1.0 s |
| Total time | ~4 s | ~4.5 s | ~3.5 s |
| GPU usage | High | High | High |

Although browser-based ASR offers faster response times, its recognition accuracy is generally lower than that of cloud-based APIs, especially in challenging scenarios. In particular, voice activity detection (VAD) must be handled separately, and the system does not perform well when users interrupt or speak over each other. Due to these limitations, we ultimately did not adopt browser-based ASR in our final implementation.

## 6 Future Work

From an application perspective, virtual avatars demonstrate tremendous potential as a new generation of human-computer interfaces. This technology enables natural language interaction with users and combines realistic facial expressions, movements, and emotional feedback, making digital services more human-centric. For example, as personalized marketing agents, virtual avatars can patiently and meticulously introduce products based on user needs and preferences, guiding users through the marketing funnel to enhance interaction experience and conversion rates. Such interaction reduces the burden on human customer service and provides 24/7 uninterrupted service, making enterprise marketing more efficient and flexible.

In addition, virtual avatars are highly suitable for applications in the health assistant domain. Users can interact with virtual avatars at any time for physical health or psychological stress to receive companionship and emotional support. Virtual avatars can record users' health status and emotional changes and provide timely suggestions based on conversation content, helping users develop good habits or seek professional assistance. As society ages and the number of elderly living alone and chronic patients continues to rise, virtual avatars can become caring companions in daily life, offering emotional comfort and health management, reducing loneliness, and improving quality of life.

Overall, virtual avatars are a technological innovation and a key driver of humanized digital services. With ongoing advances in speech recognition, natural language processing, and virtual animation technologies, the future applications of virtual avatars in marketing, healthcare, education, companionship, and other fields will become even more widespread, making them an indispensable component of a smart society.

Although the rendering workflow can achieve highly realistic virtual avatar animation and interaction, there is still a certain degree of resource inefficiency. In particular, real-time Rendering and streaming on the server side require significant GPU resources. As concurrent users increase, server load rises rapidly, leading to higher operational costs and scalability challenges.

We believe applying efficient 3D rendering technologies such as Gaussian Splatting on the client side—enabling web rendering directly in the browser—would bring significant benefits. Gaussian Splatting offers real-time Rendering and high image quality while demanding relatively low computational resources, making it well-suited for end devices. This architecture can significantly reduce server-side computational load, allowing the same backend resources to serve more users and lowering cloud GPU rental costs, thereby improving system cost-effectiveness.

Moreover, offloading rendering tasks to the client side also reduces bandwidth consumption for audio-visual streaming, enhancing the immediacy and smoothness of interactions. The client only needs to receive key animation parameters or point cloud data to complete high-quality avatar rendering locally, which is highly attractive for large-scale deployment and cross-platform applications. With the maturity of front-end graphics technologies such as WebGL and WebGPU, implementing Gaussian Splatting rendering in browsers is now feasible. This improves user experience and lays a technical foundation for the large-scale adoption and popularization of virtual avatar services.

## References

1. Bashirov, R., et al.: MoRF: mobile realistic fullbody avatars from a monocular video. In: Proceedings of the IEEE/CVF Winter Conference on Applications of Computer Vision, pp. 3545–3555 (2024)
2. Chan, E.R., et al.: Efficient geometry-aware 3D generative adversarial networks. In: Proceedings of the IEEE/CVF Conference on Computer Vision and Pattern Recognition, pp. 16123-16133 (2022)
3. Cho, K., et al.: Gaussiantalker: real-time talking head synthesis with 3D gaussian splatting. In: Proceedings of the 32nd ACM International Conference on Multimedia, pp. 10985–10994 (2024)
4. Gafni, G., Thies, J., Zollhofer, M., Niessne, M.: Dynamic neural radiance fields for monocular 4D facial avatar reconstruction. In: Proceedings of the IEEE/CVF Conference on Computer Vision and Pattern Recognition, pp. 8649–8658 (2021)
5. Giebenhain, S., Kirschstein, T., Rünz, M., Agapito, L., Niessne, M.: NPGA: Neural Parametric Gaussian Avatars. SIGGRAPH Asia,: Conference Papers (SA Conference Papers' 24), December 3–6. Tokyo, Japan (2024)
6. Grassal, P.-W., Prinzler, M., Leistner, T., Rother, C., Niessne, M., Thies, J.: Neural head avatars from monocular RGB videos. In: Proceedings of the IEEE/CVF Conference on Computer Vision and Pattern Recognition, pp. 18653–18664 (2022)
7. Li, J., Zhang, J., Bai, X., Zhou, J., Gu, L.: Efficient region-aware neural radiance fields for high-fidelity talking portrait synthesis. In: Proceedings of the IEEE/CVF International Conference on Computer Vision, pp. 7568–7578 (2023)
8. Ma, S., Weng, Y., Shao, T., Zhou, K.: . 3D gaussian blendshapes for head avatar animation. In: ACM SIGGRAPH 2024 Conference Papers, pp. 1–10 (2024)
9. Ma, Z., Zhu, X., Qi, G.-J., Lei, Z., Zhang, L.: Otavatar: one-shot talking face avatar with controllable tri-plane rendering. In Proceedings of the IEEE/CVF Conference on Computer Vision and Pattern Recognition, pp. 16901–16910 (2023)
10. Park, K., et al.: Nerfies: deformable neural radiance fields. In: Proceedings of the IEEE/CVF International Conference on Computer Vision, pp. 5865–5874 (2021)
11. Pavlakos, G., et al.: Expressive body capture: 3D hands, face, and body from a single image. In: Proceedings of the IEEE/CVF Conference on Computer Vision and Pattern Recognition, pp. 10975–10985 (2019)
12. Peng, Z., et al.: SyncTalk: the devil is in the synchronization for talking head synthesis. In: Proceedings of the IEEE/CVF Conference on Computer Vision and Pattern Recognition, pp. 666–676 (2024)

13. Qian, Z., Wang, S., Mihajlovic, M., Geiger, A., Tang, S.: 3DGS-Avatar: animatable avatars via deformable 3D gaussian splatting. In: Proceedings of the IEEE/CVF Conference on Computer Vision and Pattern Recognition, pp. 5020–5030 (2024)
14. Shen, S., Li, W., Zhu, Z., Duan, Y., Zhou, J., Lu, J.: Learning dynamic facial radiance fields for few-shot talking head synthesis. In: European Conference on Computer Vision Springer, pp. 666–682 (2022)
15. Shen, S., et al.: DiffTalk: crafting diffusion models for generalized audio-driven portraits animation. In Proceedings of the IEEE/CVF Conference on Computer Vision and Pattern Recognition, pp. 1982–1991 (2023)
16. Sun, J., et al.:. Next3D: generative neural texture rasterization for 3D-aware head avatars. In: Proceedings of the IEEE/CVF Conference on Computer Vision and Pattern Recognition, pp. 20991–21002 (2023)
17. WANG, L., et al.: StyleAvatar: real-time photorealistic portrait avatar from a single video. In: ACM SIGGRAPH 2023 Conference Proceedings, pp. 1–10 (2023)
18. Xu, Y., Su, Z., Wu, Q., Liu, Y.: GPHM: gaussian parametric head model for monocular head avatar reconstruction (2024). arXiv preprint arXiv:2407.15070
19. Xu, Y., Wang, L., Zhao, X., Zhang, H., Liu, Y.: AvatarMAV: fast 3D head avatar reconstruction using motion-aware neural voxels. In: ACM SIGGRAPH 2023 Conference Proceedings, pp. 1–10 (2023)
20. Xu, Y., et al.: LatentAvatar: learning latent expression code for expressive neural head avatar. In: ACM SIGGRAPH 2023 Conference Proceedings, pp. 1-10 (2023)
21. YE, Z., et al.: MimicTalk: mimicking a personalized and expressive 3D talking face in minutes (2024). arXiv preprint arXiv:2410.06734
22. YU, W., et al.: NOFA: NeRF-based one-shot facial avatar reconstruction. In: ACM SIGGRAPH 2023 Conference Proceedings, pp. 1–12 (2023)
23. Zhao, X., Wang, L., Sun, J., Zhang, H., Suo, J., Liu, Y.: HAvatar: high-fidelity head avatar via facial model conditioned neural radiance field. ACM Trans. Graph. **43**(1), 1–16 (2023)
24. Zhuang, Y., Zhu, H., Sun, X., Cao, X.: MofaNeRF: morphable facial neural radiance field. In: European Conference on Computer Vision Springer, pp. 268–285 (2022)

# Author Index

**C**
Chen, KuoHsiung   110

**D**
Dellinger, Andrew   110
Doan, Truong Cong   28
Duc, Phan Thanh   28

**G**
Gu, Xuze   14, 37, 82
Guo, Songliang   50

**J**
Jing, Ran   66

**L**
Liu, Xinfu   50

**M**
Ma, Fuchen   50

**P**
Pan, Xiuqin   14, 37, 82

**S**
Shen, Ao   14

**T**
Tu, Geng   66

**V**
Van Loi, Tran   28

**W**
Wang, Xiaoling   95
Wang, Yiqun   37
Wang, Zhushan   14
Wu, FuChe   110
Wu, Yirui   50

**X**
Xu, Ruifeng   66

**Z**
Zhang, Kunjing   3
Zhang, Shuyun   82

MIX
Papier aus verantwortungsvollen Quellen
Paper from responsible sources
FSC® C105338

If you have any concerns about our products,
you can contact us on
**ProductSafety@springernature.com**

In case Publisher is established outside the EU,
the EU authorized representative is:
**Springer Nature Customer Service Center GmbH
Europaplatz 3, 69115 Heidelberg, Germany**

Printed by Libri Plureos GmbH
in Hamburg, Germany